Interactive Assessment: Teachers, Parents, and Students as Partners

Interactive Assessment: Teachers, Parents, and Students as Partners

Robert J. Tierney
Thomas P. Crumpler
Cynthia D. Bertelsen
Ernest L. Bond

Christopher–Gordon Publishers

Norwood, Massachusetts

Credits

Table of Contents

Preface

The title of this book, *Interactive Assessment: Teachers, Parents, and Students as Partners*, has shifted and evolved from several drafts and earlier versions of the text to its present form. As we revised this title from a longer, more descriptive one to a shorter, more focused version, our thinking about assessment as reflected in these chapters was shifting and focusing as well. On one level, paring and tightening a manuscript so that it is conceptually coherent, well organized, and closely edited is a normal part of publishing. However, if writing is understood as a mode of learning, this process can provide opportunities for an author or authors to see their subject more deeply. Writing this book has allowed us to see the complexities of assessment and the challenges of collaboration more deeply.

Our understanding of assessment is interactive. This interaction centers around our views of partnerships that include students, teachers, parents, and other caregivers who play a role in crafting and supporting assessment that is attentive to teaching and learning. Further, while this interaction is a key feature of assessment practices that are developed in classrooms, it cannot end there. Interactive assessment moves beyond classroom walls to encompass conversations that we hope will take place around kitchen tables when children and their parents or caregivers are reviewing the school day. We believe assessment can become a topic that is a feature of literacy learning, as important yet as comfortable as talking about what books are being read, what is happening in science, or what mathematics is being studied. In short, we want to transform assessment from a test that is only given to measure outcomes to an interactive process of conversation that informs teaching and learning, encourages self-monitoring of progress and achievement, and opens space for ongoing goal setting. We hope this book fuels such conversations.

Our understanding of collaboration has deepened as well. Each of us has worked numerous hours on sections of this book to merge our different voices and philosophies of assessment into a form that achieves unity yet honors diversity. Additionally, recognizing that our voices and philosophies have been shaped by collaborations with teachers, students, colleagues, spouses, and others who continually help to challenge and refine our thinking reminds us that collaborative work is always a dialogue. That dialogue is not only the conversations and negotiations among us as authors but also the dialogue within ourselves, and with the multitude of voices that inform our thinking and imagining.

Assessment as an interactive, collaborative enterprise that involves potentially rich conversations around artifacts closely linked to students' daily work is threaded through the chapters of this book. We believe these conversations must be anchored in views of what learners actually do— the artifacts that are developed from classroom work. Our hope is that this thread functions as both an organizational theme and a catalyst to spur readers who are interested in reforming the ways they think about and develop assessment practices. Finally, we encourage readers to think about the recursive nature of conceptualizing assessment and practicing assessment with learners. Thinking and doing are inseparable in interactive assessment, and it is within this relationship that we see exciting possibilities for real and sustained change in the ways we develop assessment.

Acknowledgments

This book has been a wonderful collaboration involving ongoing conversations face to face, by telephone calls, and via a website. The conversations began with Tom and then extended to Ernie and Cynthia and later included others, especially Jane Bresler and Carolyn Cutler. I want to thank all of them for their friendship and willingness to support the vision and realization of the book. There were also some wonderful educators to whom we refer throughout the book. Thanks especially to Barbara Loar, Tammy Harper and Catherine Thome, individuals who were willing to share their insights, their wonderful explorations of practice, and their search for new possibilities. Finally, we thank Hiram Howard and Sue Canavan for their support and patience as we talked about the book and now see it realized. The book also emerged as a result of the extraordinary support of my partner, Theresa Rogers. Her insightful comments, challenges, as well as ongoing conversations around educational issues, parenting, and relationships undergird many of the notions in this book. Finally, I would like to thank my sons, Shaun and Christopher, who provided me new ways of seeing and living.

Rob Tierney

Many people have contributed to the completion of this book. The opportunity to work with fellow authors Rob, Cindy, and Ernie has truly been a privilege. Rob Tierney has been a generous mentor and friend beginning with my doctoral work and continuing as I developed my own goals and voice as an educator and researcher. His perseverance to see this project to its fruition is a model for me. Cindy and Ernie have been my friends and colleagues for over 5 years now. Each of them has brought strengths and talents to this work that have made it an enjoyable learning process. To the teachers whose voices inform this book, I thank you for the professional commitment and care you provide the children you teach. It is through your efforts that assessment will change. Finally, I need to acknowledge the support of my family, Ann, Dillon, and Peter, who have helped make my efforts possible.

Thomas Crumpler

I am constantly inspired by the efforts of both the coauthors of this book and the teachers who have offered us access to their classrooms and their insights. My graduate students at Salisbury University also deserve recognition for sharing my enthusiasm and for actually incorporating these assessment ideas into their K–12 classrooms. Thanks to Margaret for all her support. Finally, I should acknowledge my children, Nic and Nathan who give me great impetus to explore ways of improving learning and assessment.

Ernest Bond

I offer a special thank you to Jane Bresler for her ongoing support and assistance throughout the work on this project. I extend my appreciation to several individuals, first and foremost to Rob Tierney, whose support and encouragement have directed me throughout my tenure as a graduate student and young faculty member. His knowledge, expertise, and guidance have allowed me to grow as a professional in this field, far beyond my initial expectations. I would also like to convey my sincere appreciation to the teachers, parents, and students who so willingly gave of their time and shared their classrooms with us. We have learned much by being part of their learning communities.

Cynthia Bertelsen

Background

We hope that you find this book to be a valuable resource for expanding your thinking about assessment as well as a tool for more effective decision making. For ourselves, the book and accompanying CD-ROM have their antecedents in our explorations, observations, research, writing, and countless conversations with each other as well as a larger set of colleagues. On the CD-ROM, you will find a bibliography of articles, books, and Internet resources that informed our thinking, along with a lengthy report of the research initiative that served as the foundation for our thoughts. The report details our examination of various assessment reform efforts at the district, school, and individual teacher level amid the legislative assessment reform initiatives that occurred in the United States over the last 15 years

How Did This Project Begin?

The current book has several antecedents:

- The portfolio efforts that led to the book by Tierney, Carter, and Desai (1991).
- A number of dissertation studies with connections to these efforts (e.g., Carter, 1992; Crumpler, 1996; Fenner, 1995).
- Ongoing concern that assessment reform extend to report mechanisms in schools.
- A series of pursuits described below exploring report card reform efforts.

- The initiation of a study group around assessment issues that began with Tom Crumpler and Rob Tierney and expanded to include Cynthia Bertelsen, Ernest Bond, and later, Jane Bresler.

About 5 years ago, Rob Tierney and Tom Crumpler began to look into report card practices and how they aligned with attempts to reform assessment. This preliminary inquiry included research into the history of report cards in the United States and a survey of school districts across the state of Ohio to determine which ones were shifting their report card practices, which ones were attempting to reform assessments, and how these two might relate. What they found were about a dozen districts that were actively pursuing reform in varying degrees and capacities. However, they also found that many schools characterized themselves as overburdened by new standards that called for assessment reform but offered little direction in terms of staff development to support classroom teachers' efforts to shift the ways they assess learners. They began to recognize a need for a more detailed understanding of the schools that were attempting assessment reform. From the survey, 12 schools were identified2 and arrangements were made to visit these sites and to interview administrators, teachers, students, and parents to get a better understanding of how and to what degree assessment reform was taking place.

At this point Cynthia Bertelsen, Ernie Bond, and Jane Bresler joined the project as co-researchers to help conduct research at the school sites. As a team of researchers, we visited each of the schools to gather data on both the processes and the products (e.g., the documents that had been or were being produced). This second layer of our work aided us in pulling together a group of cases of reform efforts and identifying patterns and reform trends among schools. While we did not find any one "best way" to proceed, we did recognize key features that seemed to facilitate and support assessment reform (Bertelsen, Tierney, Crumpler, Bond, & Bresler, 1997). One thing we learned from this second layer of the project was a continuing need to narrow our lens. We knew the general assessment landscape as populated by individuals and institutions that were interested in shifting assessment practices. We also knew that some schools were negotiating changes in types and uses of assessments, and some were even revamping their grading systems as a way to more closely connect teaching and learning. However, we did not have a clear picture of how classroom teachers were working out some of the changes we had observed on a daily basis with learners, parents, and other caregivers. To gain a clearer sense of what was happening, we focused our work on several classrooms with the purpose of looking closely at some examples of successful assessments at work.

How Did We Change and Become Aware of Our Need to Change?

It was within a third layer of our work that we began to realize we needed some more inclusive ways to think and talk about assessment. Through ongoing e-mail conversations, conference calls, and work sessions, we began to conceptualize how assessment was embedded within larger communities and the types of networks that informed these communities. We considered how we might develop a model that would build on what teachers were doing in classrooms and that would also bring students and parents into conversations about assessment in more meaningful ways.

What emerged for us was the construct of assessment partnership or relationship that is the foundation of this book. What helped raise our own awareness and push our thinking about assessment was coming to terms with its complexity while simultaneously understanding the need to encourage teachers to develop assessments with stakeholders.

What Sustained Us?

What sustained us was a belief in the value of this work and a collegiality that cut across geographic and conceptual borders. As indicated in the preface, we brought to the collaboration diverse views of assessment and its place in schools and classrooms. It seemed to be our overarching goal of honoring the dynamic nature of assessment and uncovering ways of allowing all the voices involved space to participate that kept us writing, thinking, revising, and rethinking as we brought this manuscript to completion.

What Are Our Key Ideas?

As discussed in the first two chapters of this book, we propose that assessment efforts be examined in terms of an ethic not unlike that espoused by social scientists and caregivers—namely, that assessment should be done *with* the stakeholders rather than *to* them. For many of us, this shift to a more interactive and shared decision making entails a change in roles and relationships with students and their parents. Figure B-1 shows how the shift might appear if it were diagrammed.

**Figure B-1. Changing Roles and Relationships in the Shift
to Interactive and Shared Decision Making**

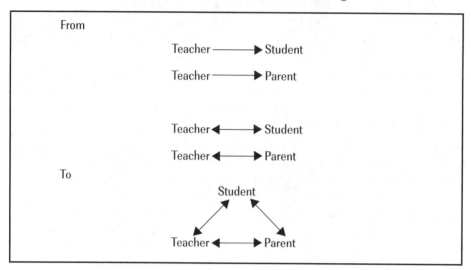

From the student's perspective, his or her learning (including learning to be a decision maker) occurs in the company of and support of others—parents, caregivers, teachers, peers, and other contributors. Whether the student is doing a project, engaged in problem solving, or participating in discovery or communication, the student or learner is engaged in learning and in learning to learn, including reflection and planning. The partnership is ongoing from the outset of schooling and should pervade all aspects of learning, including assessment.

For many of us, this entails a change in roles and relationships with students, their parents, caregivers, and interested parties that represents a different set of values than has tended to exist in the past. As our figure suggests, the shift to interactive assessments involves a change in how the teacher, student, and parent relate to one another. One way to think about the change in relationship is to recognize that we are asking teachers to engage with parents as colleagues in what might be considered an interdisciplinary research team. Parents are experts on the child's life history, whereas the teacher is an expert on pedagogy, child development, and other school-related concerns. Both experts contribute their knowledge to the team's efforts to support the success of the student. The student is apprenticed to this team, learning from both experts how to take responsibility for his or her lifelong education.

The shift in practices means that the teachers and parents, together with the student, look over the student's progress as they celebrate achievements, wrestle with problems, and engage in ongoing planning. Just as a research team might discuss what is occurring or has occurred in the past, so students, their parents, and teachers have periodic checks to examine what students have been doing in classes or projects through discussions of portfolios, dossiers, or other materials.

It is a movement from a teacher or school system prescribing what will occur to teacher, student, and others planning and making decisions together, including decisions around learning and goals. In suggesting such a shift, we are not saying that teachers do not have particular expertise and responsibilities. However, we recognize that parents, caregivers, and students also have expertise and that we must be mindful that the decisions are their decisions, or decisions about and for them.

Instead of holding parents and interested parties at arm's length, our goal is to support their contributing to the decision making process. In other words, decision making does not occur within the confines of the teacher's mind or institution, but in concert with ongoing conversations and negotiations with caregivers, the learners themselves, and others.

Our goals for classrooms suggest that the response of the teacher and the principal reflect a difference in a core goal for learning and the reasons why we repeatedly emphasize the notion of relationship and partnership. It is as if the shift involves removing the boundary of school and moving beyond teacher as guide to teacher as fellow learner with students, caregivers, and other interested parties.

How Do These Ideas Relate to the Ideas of Other Educational Researchers?

Our current view of assessment reform is consistent with Johnston's notion that "assessment . . . is based on power relationships inherent in an organized system that is embedded in, and a reflection of, societal relationships" (Johnston, 1993, p. 24) Therefore, to change assessment practice substantially is to change social practice and may entail a shift in social relationship—a change in the terms of the partnership among school, parents, students, and others. Such a change entails rethinking assessment as a learning space within which all interested parties negotiate their ongoing relationships and pursuits. It also entails reconsidering the nature of research on reform efforts, linking them to a new ethic and a new standard for validity. Perhaps we began with a rather simple-minded view of assessment reform as just a matter of adopting a new procedure—that is, simply the substitution of one practice for another. However, we began to see the importance of the relationship of any new practice to existing norms and expectations of stakeholders and the institutions that license change. As we peeled back the layers involved in reforming assessment or derailing such efforts, we became increasingly aware of assessment being stymied as a result of preexisting norms and expectations. These norms and expectations seemed to reinforce assessment as ritualistic and maintaining the power of certain groups over others—in particular, signifying the authority of the institution of schooling. We posit that once the various parties address what they deem to be needed changes in assessment practice, the reform is likely to become mutated or disappear unless it goes deeper than just a change in practice. In other words, traces of the old practices will remain and override the new.

We see our notions as reflecting Bruner's (1990) notion that a democratic society "demands that we be conscious of how we come to our knowledge and be as conscious as we can be about the values that lead us to our perspectives. It asks us to be accountable for how and what we know" (p. 31). In addition, we see it as aligned with the notion of responsive evaluation that Guba and Lincoln (1989) as well as others (e.g., Stake, 1983; Lather, 1986) have espoused. It is consistent with the notions of Moss and Schutz (2001) of creating a vibrant dialogue that allows multiple perspectives to percolate rather than be subdued and ignored—especially when the stakes are high and consensus-driven initiatives may override alternative and equally viable decisions. In terms of standards, it encourages ongoing conversations and emerging possibilities rather than fixed and a priori expectations. As Carini (1994) explained,

> In these climates, standards aren't absent; neither are they singular, nor reduced and coded as a measuring stick. In these climates, standards are active, fresh, emergent in work and works, arising in the midst of persons whose lives and works are mutually influencing, who argue and jostle or challenge each other. These are standards in a state of volatility. (p. 40)

Our work on assessment partnership has also been influenced by many colleagues who have been involved in investigations of student self-assessment (Carter, 1992), rubrics and student conferencing (Fenner, 1995), the problems with traditional methods of grading students and characterizing their development (e.g., Kohn, 1993), some of the limitations of high-stakes assessment (e.g., Hoffman, Assaf, & Paris, 2001; Madaus, 1988) and aspects of student-centered and inquiry-driven assessment (e.g., Black & William, 1998; Davies, 2000; Serafini, 2001; Short, Harste, & Burke, 1995; Stiggins, 1997). This book has to do with learning—learning to assess learning in responsive ways, how learning is intertwined with assessment, and how at times learning and assessment are indistinguishable from one another. This book is linked to views of learning that recognize the importance of learning as a team, learning with the support of others, learning from others, and helping others learn. In many ways, it builds upon a growing body of educational scholarship, particularly in the areas of communities of learning, advances in assessment theory, redefinition of educational research, institutional identity and power, school reform, and parental involvement.

Reflections on Sustaining Reform

Writing this book has shifted the way we think about assessment. Central to this shift is a vision in which students, teachers, parents, and other caregivers become partners in developing assessment relationships that support ongoing goal setting and decision making around students' literacy growth. Throughout these chapters, we have framed our beliefs and practices around this precept with the purposes of starting conversations with others who may be interested in shifting their assessment practices toward a partnership model. We view these conversations as imperative if stakeholders desire to reform assessment within classrooms, schools, and communities. However, we are not naive enough to believe that changes can happen without a commitment to seeing reforms through from conceptualization to actual implementation with learners. In our own courses and work with schools, we continue to refine and tailor our thinking about the complexities surrounding assessment. We view this type of progressive refinement as a feature of dynamic, partner-oriented assessment. We hope that colleagues who are interested in pursuing some of these same assessment goals will build this notion into frameworks they develop to fit the communities in which they work.

One key to sustaining shifts in assessment is critically reflecting upon the process or journey undertaken. In this last section, we reflect on our journey, including some of the side roads and paths that seemed promising at first but turned out to be wrong for our purposes. We hope these comments will encourage those who are considering a similar journey of their own.

Part I

Assessment and Alternatives

One

An Invitation to Assessment Reform

Introduction

In most of our everyday interactions in the world we expect to be involved in joint decision making. In legal matters, for example, we seek advice from an attorney who outlines options and possible ways to proceed. When ill, we see a doctor who gives advice as to medication and whether we need to see a specialist. In each of these brief scenarios, an assessment is made. We are aware of what is at stake and expect to be part of the decision making process, part of a conversation. However there is more going on in these situations than might be visible at first glance. On another level, each of these examples involves inquiry and negotiation. Each conversation involves inquiry into a question about health or legal options. From there, we may need to negotiate about the necessity of a medical procedure or the best course to protect one's rights as a citizen. Further, we could pursue other opinions about each of these issues, weigh them against one another, and decide what is best.

In a similar fashion, we might expect schools in which assessment is central to a child's future to engage parents, caregivers, and teachers in conversations that lead to joint decision making informed by inquiry and negotiation. We might further expect these schools to cultivate partnerships committed to developing assessments that allow students to demonstrate growth and achievement. However, when we visit schools and classrooms we do not find many conversations in the context of assessment reform. For example, we have worked in schools where teachers have attempted to pursue shifts in assessment through use of student-led conferences tied to portfolios. Yet, the types of conversations that promote partnerships we see as necessary to shift assessment and improve teaching and learning seem to be lacking.

Recently, more traditional forms of testing such as proficiency and other norm-referenced tests have come to be termed as high stakes, while alternative or learner-centered assessments that inform instruction such as portfolios and literacy profiles are designated as not involving high stakes. Our own work and thinking about these issues has led us to believe that all assessment is high stakes if we acknowledge that decisions affecting children and their futures are informed by these assessments. In fact we argue that whether assessments are formative or summative[1], whether they involve planning for instruction or determining grades, whether they are used to sort learners into tracks or decide eligibility for grade-level advancement or graduation, there is always a great deal at stake. In our view, this is part of the nature of assessment itself.

What is missing from current conversations about assessment reform is an emphasis on assessment partnerships and inquiry in assessment. The partnerships we imagine include teachers, parents and other caregivers, students, school administrators, and others who come together with the purpose of developing assessments that support teaching and learning and encourage joint decision making. This development should be viewed as part of a larger process of inquiry in which both process and goals are valued. Mutual respect, connectedness to curriculum, and a recognition that all the partners can contribute to a learning community inform these partnerships and support this type of inquiry. Central to our vision is a belief in the importance of trust. This trust must be nurtured as teachers work with students, parents, and caregivers. We believe that these new partnerships will provide opportunities for reimagining learning communities where inquiry is both a belief and a practice. These partnerships must begin at the classroom level with support from schools and districts if they are to be successful.

The Challenges of Shifting Assessment

The shift in reform that we propose in this book involves new ways of looking at assessment through two lenses: partnership and community, and self-assessment. Using these as frames, we describe ways to develop and refine assessment practices that engage students, teachers, and parents or caregivers in ongoing description, reflection, negotiation, and goal setting. Most importantly, these practices are collaborative, and this collaborative process is informed by a belief in inquiry. Through collaborative inquiry we imagine the development of partnerships committed to fair and just assessment within dynamic learning communities that value multiple possibilities. We know reform is difficult and that the work of forging new partnerships and creating new communities is also difficult. We hope that teachers who are considering changing the ways they assess students will find this book useful as they conceptualize and implement this rewarding work.

Pursuing Assessment Reform

With these two lenses, partnership and community, as focal points, we identified some issues for students, teachers, parents, and other stakeholders interested in assessment. We recast these issues as challenges for those initiating, developing, refining, and sustaining assessment reform.

Through the lens of partnership there are four challenges:

- developing relationships in assessment that are transactional
- reconceptualizing assessment relationships as richly interactive
- shifting expectations from primarily outcomes to ongoing refinement in which learners have a sense of ownership of their growth and goals
- developing assessment in service of learning

Through the lens of community, there are three challenges:

- negotiating with stakeholders to achieve a new democratic and participatory community
- recognizing and honoring diverse examples of growth and achievement over time
- supporting teachers, parents, and students engaged in thoughtful assessment within constraints of standards and other frameworks.

Shifting the focus of assessment from more traditional systems, which emphasize product, toward systems that honor both process and product, necessitates thinking critically and differently about assessment. In more traditional assessment practices such as standardized testing and multiple-choice style, teacher-constructed assessments, issues such as objectivity and comparability have been significant, while the learners' voices have been silenced and ignored. In more learner-based assessments such as portfolios, conferences, and other performance assessments objectivity is displaced by an emphasis on the individual's growth over time.

As assessment practices shift towards looking at growth over time, the learner's voice becomes paramount for developing the partnerships we envision. Learners use their voices to narrate the story of their own achievements and participate in community building within schools and classrooms. This narrative, which includes individual student's written reflections as well as student-teacher conferences, provides ways for learners to describe and interpret their own growth and achievement based on samples of their own work.

In our view, discussions about how self-assessment narratives, both written and oral, should be woven into the process of constructing a classroom community. This led us to wonder how to create reflective space to consider individual strengths, given the nature of traditional power dynamics informing assessment. We noted even less discussion about how these assessments such as portfolios or exhibitions and their accompanying narratives might displace report cards. We wondered whether traditional report cards represent student learning and achievement in ways that can inform instruction. Finally, as we advocate for visions and possibilities for change in assessment practices that include report card reform, we envision not only the processes to more richly assess what students are capable of as learners but also the ways we might represent that knowledge.

An Invitation

One of our goals for suggesting new partnerships and stronger communities is to help teachers think about more effective ways to work within the system by encouraging what actually can be done. We are not prescribing the way for classroom teachers to reform assessment. Rather, we offer guidelines and resources to assist teachers interested in shifting assessments toward a more interactive model. Based on this goal, we do not necessarily advocate for wholesale change or abandoning practices that teachers have found successful. We do believe that our approach is communicative, collaborative, and centered on learning goals—in essence, helping students learn to learn. We see these new assessment partnerships and evolving communities centered around closely linking teaching and learning, empowering learners to self-assess, and increasing conversations among students, teachers, and parents or other caregivers who have a stake in a child's literacy growth.

For us, this book has been both a conversation and a journey of historical analyses, investigating successful teaching practices, chasing down leads about promising assessment techniques, developing presentations for schools and conferences, and, finally, reconsidering our own views on the nature of assessment. We invite you to read this book as travelers seeking new vistas and possibilities for developing assessments that support and challenge learners as well as inform and extend teaching. We encourage travelers to ask questions, test possibilities, and strike out on their own as they read this text. We hope that along the way interesting and useful practices for assessing learners will emerge. We imagine partnerships and envision communities that view assessment as an opportunity for learners to inquire, grow, and change within contexts of safety and support. From these contexts, we believe learners can map new ways to achieve meaningful goals.

Our own experiences in trying to shift assessment practices and reform assessment systems have shown that efforts must begin with four questions. First, what is the purpose of shifting assessment practices? Second, who are the stakeholders or key players that need to be informed and consulted? Third, who will help initiate and sustain these shifts as they unfold in schools and classrooms? Finally, what types of practices might be implemented that will foster the types of partnerships and communities that are critical to assessment reform?

In the following chapters, we discuss and suggest practical strategies for teacher-led and student-led conferences, describe the usefulness of narratives for assessing learning, evaluate some current technologies for assessment, and explore the complex issues of grading. In each chapter, we include examples that will help teachers and others see possibilities for initiating change and suggest ways to sustain these changes. In each section, we begin with the most familiar and move toward the unfamiliar. The artifacts section, for example, begins with how to write narrative assessments, which is likely to be a familiar assessment form. The section continues with less familiar forms, including the report dossier and digital forms of assessments. The section on conversations begins with variations on the parent-teacher conference and moves toward the possibilities inherent in student-led conferences. That section concludes with a "troubleshooting" chapter on handling problems that arise in human relationships.

We think classrooms and schools in which assessment is inseparable from teaching and learning can pursue these reforms and that the time is right for such pursuits. We hope this book will help all stakeholders take first or next steps on the journey to building positive relationships in the interest of helping students become independent learners.

Endnotes

1   By formative assessment, we mean assessment that is ongoing, and considers process as a key feature of learning. Summative assessment refers to evaluation that focuses primarily on outcomes.

TWO

Benchmarking, Grading, Comparing, and Conversing

Introduction

There is an old adage that simple answers to complex questions may be appealing but are usually wrong. Certainly, this seems true when you consider attempts to describe and summarize student achievement. Letter grades, descriptors such as improving or emerging, checklists, rubrics, and continua represent simple, widely accepted ways to characterize performance. Unfortunately, they are apt to mischaracterize the complexities of achievement.

There are several reasons that these descriptors are problematic. First, the nature of student development is multidimensional and less uniform than tests would suggest. Just as children grow at different rates and may spurt at different ages, so student learning develops at different rates and in accordance with different patterns. Consider the following patterns for students learning a task such as snowboarding. Student 1 might be successful immediately and improve steadily, Student 2 might have some difficulty and then learn smoothly, and Student 3 might be alternately successful and frustrated.

As Figure 2-1 suggests, student learning is multifaceted and at times erratic. Each student's profile differs from those of other students and will likely change over time in different ways. Figures 2-2 and 2-3 graphically illustrate changes over time in activity and student development in selected areas. As you examine the graphs, you will notice variations in books read, effective strategy use, and the students' facility with effectively setting goals. The four students start at different points, and each student's progress over time varies.

Figure 2-1. Percentage of Successful Snowboard Runs

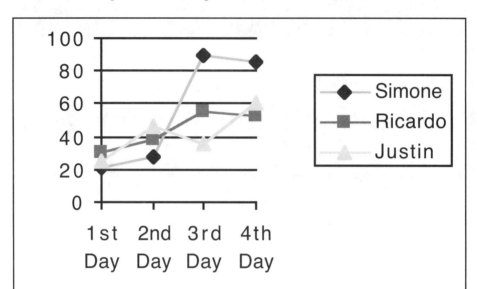

Figure 2-2. End of Session 1

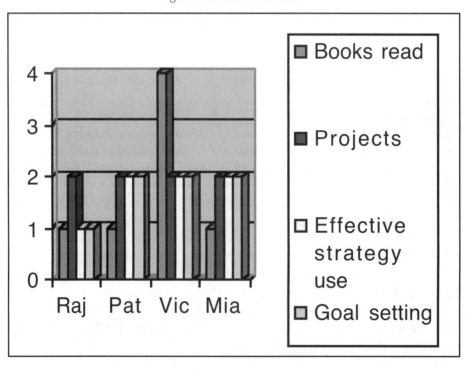

Figure 2-3. End of Session 2

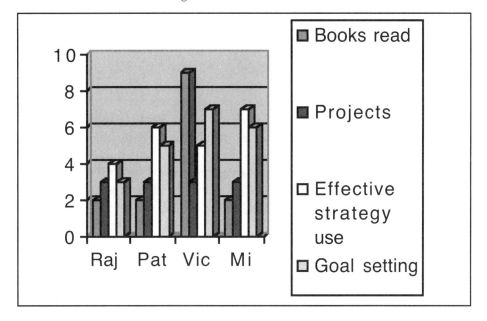

Even if we could represent development graphically, there would be enormous differences over time. We might compare development to a series of urban landscapes, with each landscape differing from other landscapes based on its history, geography, investment, interests, and so on.

There are other problems in describing student development. Student learning often does not lend itself to scoring, grading, or the use of uniform ways of comparing students. Scores have a tendency to give the illusion that the strategies, processes, and achievements of learning are quantifiable and comparable. Learning is difficult to describe except in a case-by-case manner with a mix of qualitative descriptions, examples, comments, and perspectives. Although summarizing the complex nature of student development is a problem that we may never fully resolve, we should not compound our problems by pretending that the scores that we derive are accurate and that developmental patterns are the same for all students.

A further problem is the tendency to rely upon single forms of measurement when multiple measures should be used, even if these measures do not yield similar results. The reality is that different forms of measurement are likely to yield different results. Indeed, most of us prefer certain kinds of assessment over others and will sometimes suggest that we would perform differently according to the circumstances. Shavelson, Baxter, and Pine (1992) compared a hands-on science curriculum and a textbook-based science program using a range of measures from multiple-choice to open-ended questions to portfolio-like assessment. It was no surprise that students were ranked differently from one measure to the next.

Medical doctors listen to what their patients say; they examine the body with their eyes, ears, and hands; and they use other technologies such as blood tests in order to ascertain the nature of the problem. They may compare the results of a new test with previous results, as when radiologists compare a new mammogram with previous ones to see if there are any changes. Good doctors want to be sure they make an accurate diagnosis so they can offer the proper treatment for the problem. Doctors know that each assessment by itself is limited. The patient can offer important clues to the problem but usually does not have the medical knowledge to interpret those clues—and, in fact, may be misinterpreting them. A physical examination offers more clues but is limited to what the doctor can see, hear, smell, and touch. Other tests that discern internal conditions provide more clues, especially when one can compare the results to previous tests, but these must also be interpreted. Does the patient have one overriding problem or are there multiple problems? What are the most prudent first steps for treatment, steps that balance relief and improvement against risk? Multiple forms of assessment help doctors to answer these questions.

Teaching is at least as complex as understanding the workings of the human body. Like doctors, we need multiple forms of assessment so that we can make good instructional decisions. Every form of educational assessment has limits, including construction, the context in which it is used, and the fact that it is a single snapshot in a complex life.

Many claims have been made about forms of school-based assessment, including assertions about the superiority of standardized forms of assessment over that which is context-dependent, selective, or subjective. Yet doctors do not eschew conversations with the patient in favor of using only blood tests and the like—if they had no notion of the patient's complaint, how would they know where to begin to look for the problem? They might seek multiple perspectives from the patient's family (another source of subjective but significant information) and combine that data with their own observations (perhaps a little less subjective, but limited in time) and other forms of tests in order to make diagnostic and treatment decisions. Like doctors, teachers note the strengths and weaknesses of each assessment and balance those strengths and weaknesses by using multiple assessments across time.

There is a tendency to oversubscribe to a model of development tied to preset criteria that are aligned with an established curriculum and an overly reductive list of features. While curriculum standards may be useful as ways to inform a teacher's observations of a student, they should not be the sole determinant of learning. A teacher needs to be poised to generate criteria linked to what students demonstrate, rather than just fitting performance to preset checklists, profiles, rubrics, and developmental sequences. It is always useful to construct categories for the checklist or rubric as they emerge as possibilities and to do so in a manner that fits with the evolution of learning. Following the student will require the use of checklists as guides or as a menu of possibilities, but not the sole determiner of what is considered.

With due consideration to these problems, let us explore some of the means of benchmarking, grading, and reporting student progress. We would stress that we do so cautiously, with the goal of engaging parents and students with the field work of learning so that they can offer perspectives that promote flexibility and adjustments on an ongoing basis. In this model, a student's learning and development are viewed as dynamic and complex rather than fixed and fitted to rigidly predetermined sequences.

At the heart of our approach are conversations between all the stakeholders in a child's educational progress—teachers, parents, and the students themselves. We believe that the development of lifelong learners requires that students take a leading role in their own assessment. We believe that teachers and parents must work together to help children learn.

We see the goal of the school as engaging parents in an assessment partnership that begins at the outset of each school year and session rather than only at the completion of schooling. In other words, parents and students can be partners in setting goals as well as studying and analyzing progress. There are many ways teachers can and do pursue these goals in their classrooms as a part of everyday classroom life and in the classroom assessment system. Whether it is placing student work in a display, holding an open house to exhibit student work, or simply sharing portfolios, there are a host of activities that offer opportunities for grand conversations in which students and those who care about them can reflect on what they have done. Two examples follow:

- On a daily basis, Marie has students share their work with the whole class and in small groups. The sharing is used sometimes to celebrate what students have done or to offer advice or feedback. Marie sees it as an opportunity to explore with students what is different about what they do and achieve. Sometimes, she will even use a flip chart to note some of these features and then have students suggest other features. Sometimes she will have students place sticky notes next to students' work (on display on bulletin boards) highlighting certain features. Marie engages parents in three ways: open houses where student work is displayed and students introduce their parents to their class work; comments accompanying student work that is sent to the home; and a student-teacher-parent conference where the teacher and parents discuss features of the students work.

- Linda has students develop their own rubrics for looking at their own and other students' work. The rubric-based analyses are used then as conversation starters about student work. Interestingly, the rubric is not where the conversation ends but where it begins. Furthermore, Linda always ends with a conversation about how well the rubric worked. Indeed, in other activities in Linda's classroom some of the richest conversations occur around what should count as criteria. To inform parents, Linda often sends the different rubrics home and encourages parents to look at their child's work in terms of the different features on the rubric and to suggest others. Linda tries to avoid over-subscribing to a single fixed rubric or a rubric that fits all students across all projects.

Such conversations become a sounding board for exploring ideas— considering the suggestions of others and seeing one's own ideas differently. They offer a means of exploring ideas and identity as well as learning from and with others. Sometimes displays, rubrics, and conversations help students and parents attain perspectives on students' work as well as enlightening them about the complexities of development, including the danger of comparing one's own work to that of others. A better, although not infallible, basis for comparison might be the students' own portfolios or samples of classroom work from previous years that demonstrate development.

Any analysis or depiction of student development is rarely straightforward and never as uncomplicated as any grading or scoring system or even rubric is likely to represent. This should not be all that surprising since assessment is rarely straightforward even if it depicts development or achievements within simple areas. Although we may hope for simplicity and even pursue ways to depict progress simply, it would be foolish to count on doing so.

Published curriculum and governmental guides often provide performance standards or enlist a scope and sequence of objectives that might be used to analyze student progress. But even authors of such lists or profiles often stress that they are intended to be suggestive rather than prescriptive, that is, as menus suggesting possibilities rather than as mandates or fixed developmental sequences. Furthermore, they suggest that analyses using such profiles need to be viewed cautiously. The *Primary Language Record* (Barrs, Ellis, Hester, & Thomas, 1988) was developed in an effort to help teachers and parents engage in conversations around the use of the various profiles and records that  are gathered on each student. They stress to teachers that the continuum is not infallible and that sharing it with parents should involve a discussion of the caveats in order to avoid the possibility that parents or teachers might oversubscribe to analyses using such profiles. Likewise, Peter Johnston (1993) makes the following recommendations in the notes that accompany a profile he offers (Table 2-1):

Explanation of the Reporting System

We encourage our teaching faculty to be descriptive rather than judgmental in their assessments of children's development because it helps them to be more focused on their teaching. However, the detailed knowledge that the teachers have of their students can be very time-consuming to write down, and possibly more than some parents might want to know. To be efficient, we have developed some categories as shorthand for describing students' literacy development. These categories are *early, emergent, maturing,* and *expanding.* Reducing children's development to these single words means trading detailed documentation for ease of reporting, which opens the possibility of misinterpretation. The following table describes the ways we are using them. (p. 318)

Table 2-1. Reading Development in the Primary Grades

Beginning	Early	Emergent	Maturing	Expanding
Participates in story reading activities Curious about print Has memory for book language Retells story to match the illustrations Knows how books work but not how words work Recognizes own name Relies on being read to	Has favorite books Consistently recognizes 5 or 6 words Independently engages with books for around 5 minutes at a time Makes connections with other books and experiences Views self as a reader Tries to match each spoken word to a written one in familiar books with one sentence per page, and tries again if the numbers don't match	Consistently recognizes 20 or more words out of context Initiates independent reading of favorite books Chooses books of appropriate difficulty Makes connection with own writing Uses initial letters along with meaning and other cues to figure out words and correct errors Still needs some support with unfamiliar texts Beginning to understand what reading can do for him/her Beginning to recognize different authors' styles	Familiar with a range of genres Attempts challenging books Thinking critically, speculating on why the author used particular words, characters, etc. Reads for learning and entertainment Mostly reads silently Beginning to use reference texts Comfortable using all letters and some analogies to figure out words Initiates conversation with others about books	Can think about own response to reading and speculate about others' responses Expects texts to have more than one meaning, and notices subtleties Reads independently for at least 45 minutes—cannot be easily distracted when in a good book Uses library independently Self-motivated, confident reader Figures out most new words

Similar profiles have been developed for all curriculum areas. For example, Beeth and his teacher colleagues (Beeth et al., 2001) developed a continuum for assessing science learning, shown in Table 2-2.

Although such rubric-based reports can offer some understanding, better yet would be a conversation between parent and teacher (and possibly involving the child—see the chapters on conferencing) that would flesh out the details of the student's development. In such conferences teachers can provide clear examples to illustrate the nature of a child's development.

We do, however, watch for children whose rate of development may be lagging in order to prevent serious problems from developing. If a child's development does not meet expectations, the teacher and parents along with administrators should come together to create a plan to diagnose, consider possibilities, and address the students needs.

Table 2-2. Sample Items From a Continuum for Science Learning

Beginning View	Developing View	Advancing View	Consolidating View
Describes objects Observes how an object interacts with its environment Asks questions about objects and phenomena	Gives more detailed descriptions of objects and possible influences Collects and organizes data and details procedures for what is done Relates explanations to observations Suggests different possibilities	Predicts how an object will behave if conditions change Locates and uses reference books and extracts information Links events into a chain or sequence Details an outcome Suggests data that might be collected to answer questions	Gives causal explanation Suggests further questions

Schools of Thought Around Development

Teachers, parents, and students need to be aware that there are different schools of thought around the nature of development. Most curriculum guides, scope and sequence listings, performance standards, and profiles suggest that development is ongoing as students master one skill and then the next or proceed from one stage to the next. Others argue that development occurs in a less linear fashion and that the developmental notions should be reconceptualized in terms of the student using his or her expertise in a flexible and refined fashion over a variety of tasks representing a range of issues and topics. In accordance with these notions, development can be seen not as mastery of subskills but as the ongoing refinement of abilities linked to long-term goals for how students handle multiple and increasingly complex situations. In the short term, a teacher might engage students in reading a single book or text to explore a topic or issue. In the long term, the teacher is intent on developing an interest in reading, pursuing connections across different books, developing curiosity in students, making comparisons across issues, refining the flexible use of strategies, and developing breadth and depth of understandings. Table 2-3 depicts some of these notions.

Table 2-3. Notions Around Development: Mastery of Skills Versus Refining Abilities

Short-term or single-instance situations	Long-term or multiple-instance situations
• Using single texts or topics	• Using a range of texts and situations in a multilayered fashion
Affect	
• Actively engaging in learning at times	• Developing various uses across a range of situations
Strategies	
• Using strategies to read a single text effectively • Probing single sources • Planning • Self-questioning • Troubleshooting • Making connections • Collaborating	• Developing strategies to make meaning; customizing strategies to meet a range of situations • Using multiple resources • Being flexible, reflective, coordinated • Linking themes across topics • Looking back, forward, and beyond • Contributing to communities via different partnerships
Outcomes	
• Knowing main idea • Knowing details • Knowing conclusions • Knowing implications • Completing a range of activities	• Developing overall understanding, intertextual connections, and themes • Producing projects • Applying knowledge
Self-Assessment	
• Self-monitoring needs and achievement • Using on-line problem solving	• Refining observations and analysis techniques • Using self-scrutiny, goal setting, and self-determinations • Developing overall goals, progress, and patterns

Most parents are concerned with their son's or daughter's achievement, whether on tests, in terms of expectations, or in comparison with others. In the interest of providing parents with such information, most schools and sometimes states or provinces will provide a report card. Usually these reports include details of expectations as well as overall test results. In some cases they note how a student compares with other students or with performance necessary to progress. Keeping parents (and students) informed is important, but we should be sure that they are well informed rather than misinformed. Parents need to be positioned to make reasonable judgments. To this end, we recommend that parents and students be given access to research papers and critiques that present different viewpoints or findings. In addition, schools might provide parents with different perspectives on various topics such as assessment, literacy, mathematics, science, or art. Some principals and teachers offer newsletters as a means of providing such information. We recommend taking the additional step of holding meetings at which parents are given the opportunity to see firsthand different tests of different types, different curricula, and so forth.

We need to open up the black box of test scores and student rankings to ensure that parents and students are aware of the assumptions and limitations of such scores. Our goal is not to have parents and students dismiss such information but to avoid their oversubscribing to its infallibility. Scores represent one source of information but should not be viewed as the sole source of information, nor even the most compelling. We hope that this book will help serve this purpose by describing practices that will develop an informed partnership among students, teachers, and parents. We are striving for methods of reporting and representing student growth that involve three-way conversations grounded in what students do, including the complexities, nuances, and idiosyncrasies of development.

A Query

So, how would you respond to the parent's question: How is she doing?

1. Her performance is average
2. She was placed 15 out of 21 students
3. She received a B
4. All of the above

We view such responses as problematic for a number of reasons. They define the student yet they do not reveal the basis on which the judgment was made. Furthermore, none of the responses are constructive in that they do not give the student or the parents information about what the child needs in order to improve. This type of assessment takes the form of an a priori judgment and therefore does not invite discussion among the parents, the student, and the teacher. Finally, these responses emphasize education as a competition among students or comparison across students as the end goal.

Ongoing Concerns

In recent years, we have seen an increased use of profiles, continua, rubrics, and other scales as vehicles for placing students developmentally. While we support their use as a way of helping gain perspective on a student's growth, we do not support their use in a lockstep fashion. Not all students develop in accordance with the descriptors that are applied or in the sequence suggested. Continua tend to assume that there is a hierarchy of skills to be developed or mastered, rather than viewing students as learning to use skills with flexibility and in increasingly refined ways as they work toward long-term goals. Although profiles and sequences provide interesting ways to inform assessments and are better than a score, they should be viewed as menus of possibilities that inform instead of as rigid checklists for how students are ranked, classified, or forced to proceed.

In her book, *Making Classroom Assessment Work*, Davies (2000) stresses,

Making classroom assessment work means reframing the conversation from one about ranking and sorting students to one about assessing learning in the context of our students' futures. It means talking with and listening to learners, their parents, and the community about learning and assessment. It means involving students and parents, giving choices, and sharing control. When it comes to classroom assessment, solutions can only be found in thoughtful, informed conversation as we work together on behalf of students and their learning. (pp. 77–78)

We prefer an ongoing approach to benchmarking, grading, comparing, and conversing. If assessment is ongoing, then it occurs from the outset of classroom explorations and activities rather than only at the completion. Assessment is something that is integrated into classroom planning and occurs from the beginning of classroom units. This model involves a number of significant shifts: that assessment should occur not at the end of activities but from the outset and throughout; that assessment should not be done *to* others but *with* them; and that assessment should be done from both inside and outside rather than be imposed from the outside.

Underlying our view of benchmarks is respect for and appreciation of diversity, a need for flexibility, and an understanding of the unpredictable shifts in what is learned and how development occurs. We would like to see far more flexibility in what criteria are used—what is assessed and how it is assessed. There is a certain volatility to what we are proposing consistent with what happens in classrooms (see Carini, 1994). It is a volatility similar to what Fenner (1995) discovered in her classroom when her fifth graders discussed each others' work in terms of the criteria from rubrics that they applied to their writings and projects. Students were learning about learning in more and more expansive ways, and in a dialectic rather than a linear manner. This type of learning and assessment occupies a different space from grades and graduaion requirements, which many students and their caregivers have accepted as convention (Crumpler, 1996). However, it is more consistent with the constructivist notion of responsive evaluation that Guba and Lincoln (1989) as well as others (e.g. Stake, 1983; Lather, 1986) have espoused:

> Responsive evaluation is not only responsive for the reason that it seeks out different stakeholder views but also since it responds to those items in the subsequent collection of information. It is quite likely that different stakeholders will hold very different constructions with respect to any particular claim, concern, or issue. As we shall see, one of the major tasks of the evaluator is to conduct the evaluation in such a way that each group must confront and deal with the constructions of all the others, a process we shall refer to as a hermeneutic dialectic. (Guba & Lincoln, 1989, p. 41).

As in "the study of interpretation" and "logical argumentation," the words "hermeneutic" and "dialectic" suggest that a conversation about assessment involves the possibility of multiple interpretations of data, and that participants would discuss these interpretations together, making arguments about possible interpretations. Earlier in the chapter, we suggested that doctors use multiple sources of data in order to draw conclusions about the nature of illness. Their sources of data may not agree; a good diagnosis comes from multiple interpretations of data rubbing up against one another until the doctor has made a logical explanation that attempts to account for all the facts that have been presented.

In the next section of this book, we present a number of assessment artifacts—narratives, report dossiers, and digital forms of assessment. The creation of these artifacts can be an ongoing part of classroom life, with even those created by teachers operating in a child-centered fashion. The third section of this book presents formats for assessment conversations among parents, teachers, and students. Many of these conversations can revolve around or incorporate assessment artifacts.

Three

Developing New Partnerships and Communities of Inquiry

Interactive Assessment and the Work of Collaboration

Collaborative work is a journey. The process of completing this project has been analogous to the approach to interactive assessment that we advocate in this text. Our journey has taken place over an extended time period, involved different voices negotiating and compromising about our goals and purposes, and included opportunities for progressive refinement of ideas and ways to represent what we really meant. We have engaged in numerous conversations about how our goals aligned with and might perhaps challenge some of the larger assumptions in the communities of schools and universities where we do our work. Our partnership as a group of authors has remained dynamic and equitable as different members have moved to new jobs and new roles and have taken on different aspects of the project. Through this process, the larger goal of developing and composing a book for teachers, parents, and others that honestly confronts the challenging work of reforming assessment reform has remained at the forefront.

Similarly, the view of assessment we present here assumes stakeholders will need to have conversations about goals and purposes for assessment. They will negotiate ways to achieve those goals and honor those purposes while remaining committed to supportive partnerships that develop strong learning communities. Within those communities, the collaborative, engaged work of assessment will inform teaching and learning. In the remainder of this book, we describe assessments that are aligned with these guidelines in detail and provide examples of assessments that could be used in classrooms.

With Emphasis on High-Stakes Testing, Can Shifts in Classroom Assessment Make Any Difference?

When the early draft of this book was reviewed, some queried the relationship of the book to traditional assessment, especially high-stakes testing. We do not think that an emphasis on high-stakes testing should preclude the pursuit of partnerships. Instead, we suggest that the decision making (e.g., promotion or retention) heightens the need for establishing a working relationship with parents and students. Parents, teachers, and students should be encouraged to make well-informed judgments and set reasonable goals based upon a discussion of various factors. We would suggest that these conversations are apt to lead to better decisions than those based on cut-off scores from a single test or decision making that excludes them. We suggest that doing anything less would be neither judicious nor ethical. Indeed, the validity of using tests for such purposes lacks what we have defined as transactional validity, unless students and parents are included in such decision making.

In the current educational climate, the need for teachers to develop partnerships around assessments that give learners opportunities to take a lead in their own growth, achievement, and goal setting is more important than ever. Teachers are closely involved with the daily interactions of students. They witness the progress and development firsthand, and they need to be closely involved in assessment as well. Yet recent changes in assessment, especially if they involve new standardized tests, have not always involved teachers. We believe that all assessments give an incomplete picture and tell an incomplete story since processes of learning are ongoing and embedded in social relationships. The challenge is not, therefore, to develop a comprehensive assessment or high-stakes test that will capture all aspects or facets of a learner's strengths and competencies. Instead, we need to develop new assessment practices that are negotiated among teachers, learners, and other partners and that will create opportunities to view rich representations of learners' abilities.

Our own investigations (Bertelsen, et al. 1997; Tierney, et al. 1998) indicate that reform in assessment has too often been implemented from the top down. In this view, control of the process is located outside the classroom and the purview of teachers. Teachers are the passive receivers of new ideas about and approaches to assessment instead of being actively involved in the construction of new types of assessments. Since the reform is initiated and controlled from the outside by administrators, curriculum directors, and others, teachers sometimes feel that one more thing is being asked of them with little or no development support. Furthermore, if the reforms involve new high-stakes tests, these tests tend to drive the curriculum as instruction becomes more closely linked to raising test scores rather than to learning.

If teachers, together with students, parents, and others, are to remain professionals and in charge of learning in schools and classrooms, they need to develop assessments that are closely tied to their work with students. These learner-centered assessments should be viewed as equally important as high-stakes tests when decisions about a child's progress, achievement, and future goals are under consideration.

Our goal is not to condemn traditional forms of testing and assessment, nor do we expect them to disappear in favor of the types of assessments we are proposing. To take this perspective at a time when teachers throughout the country are feeling the impact of testing would be in some ways unethical. What we are proposing is that reconceptualizing all assessments in terms of the partnership and community orientation we are describing will help all of us reimagine ways that assessment can better serve learners and enhance good teaching. We know such a reconceptualization will require work to shift thinking and assessment practice. However, we believe the benefits for learners will greatly outweigh the work required, and we hope that the chapters that follow will help teachers, parents, students, and others interested in assessment reform think about how to initiate and sustain change.

How Are the Proposed Assessment Shifts Aligned With Curricular Frameworks?

District and state curricula are certainly a piece of the larger learning puzzle within which teachers, parents, and students work. Viewing assessment as a process of building partnerships within the learning community helps empower teachers to think imaginatively about curricular responsibilities and to use assessment partnerships as a way to meet those responsibilities.

Assessment aspires to balance tensions between adopting a purely directive role versus a purely open role for teacher interaction with students and parents, with the goal of promoting student voice as part of the assessment processes. The curricular expectations teachers face can, in our view, provide instructional space for teachers to craft assessments as part of their instructional planning. The assessments we propose align with a variety of curricular emphases as they allow teachers to assess student learning in a variety of ways.

For example, in one first-grade classroom, the teacher developed portfolios with the children as a way to promote their ongoing literacy learning. Her goal was to create portfolios from her current instructional practices rather than impose a preset model on the students. With a university researcher as her partner, she gave the children large envelopes and asked them to either bring photographs from home to paste on their portfolios or draw their own design on the front. The university researcher had periodic conferences with the children as they added samples from their classroom work over the course of the school year.

In the final month of school, the teacher and the researcher revisited the portfolios with each child and assisted them in choosing work that represented their progress over the entire year. There was a culminating experience at which the parents, caregivers, and administrative personnel viewed the portfolios with the first-grade children.

Historically, teachers have done assessments *to* students (and their parents) rather than *with* them. The challenge for teachers is to facilitate and coach students' understanding and practice of self-assessment while resisting a more directive and less interactive role in their classrooms. For students, the challenge is to assume more responsibility for their own learning and systematically organize evidence to represent their progress. For parents and caregivers, the challenge is to enter the conversation of assessment as a supportive partner in negotiating with the child and child's teacher.

The Role of Self-Assessment in Partnerships

Trying to develop new paths and ways to more richly assess what children are doing involves constructing new strategies to represent the individual and collaborative understandings of children's learning. A central feature of this effort is the role of self-assessment. From our perspective, self-assessment has four key purposes:

- To provide learners with opportunities to systematically evaluate their own growth and development

- To engage learners in dynamic, meaningful goal setting around their own needs and desires as learners

- To enlist learners' purposeful self-assessment that contributes to an evolving community of learning

- To encourage learners to practice ongoing inquiry into their own meaning-making processes.

Self-assessment involves modeling, criteria setting, and goal setting as ways to create space for learners involved in negotiating multiple views on texts and on themselves. Each of these purposes listed above necessitates that together with students, teachers and parents regard assessment as a process that may involve reconceptualizing goals as new evidence and samples of a student's work are selected, organized, and reflected upon. In effect, the goal is to create different types of instructional spaces in which assessment is embedded within the work of the classroom as opposed to being attached to instructional sequences at the end. The types of spaces we imagine for learners allow discourses about assessment that are more exploratory and learner directed. Within these spaces, we envision conversations about texts taking place in a variety of ways so that learners better understand the complexities of really looking at and evaluating their own growth over time.

Further, we have seen how a teacher, reflecting on his or her own practices and interactions with students, can develop effective practices of self-assessment. To these purposes, we expand the concept of portfolios beyond collecting writing to include other forms of work such as models, photographs, and visual representations that encourage students to talk or to write about relationships among the different artifacts. Providing students opportunities for self-assessment that are valued by others is critical and can encourage trust among community members.

One approach to self-assessment that we believe holds great promise is ongoing conferencing. In videotaped portfolio conferences with students (Bond, Tierney, Bertelsen, & Bresler, 1997), we have seen how dynamics among students, teachers, and parents impact the depth of comments, the quality of goal setting, and the collaborative nature of assessment. Working together requires ongoing conversation to facilitate learning. This indicates how valuable teacher-led and student-led conferences can be in developing and realizing the spirit of self-assessment and partnership we have been describing. Both types of conferences necessitate rehearsals so students can practice the language of self-assessment. Teachers and parents serve in supportive and facilitative roles as they assist students in describing achievement and setting goals.

What About Issues of Reliability and Validity?

In terms of notions of validity, we find Stake's (1983) responsive evaluation to be useful in this area. It primarily involves recognizing that developing ongoing relationships among students, teachers, parents, and others key to the growth of the learner is central to assessment. The purposes of these relationships is to negotiate a variety of assessment practices that honor the multifaceted nature of learning, help set goals that continue to inform growth, reinform teaching, and create communities of learners who support and value one another. We are arguing for a shift toward a different type of validity—one we call transactional validity. With this concept, we emphasize that to be valid, or to assess what it purports to assess, assessments have to consider the give-and-take among stakeholders who develop assessments within shared understandings and provide ways for due process.

For example, a student together with teachers and others might develop an assessment relationship that facilitates collecting some type of authentic samples of the student's progress. Additionally, this provides a way to reflect upon the how and why of the collection process, selects media to represent both the samples and the process in a systematic way, and engages the stakeholders in decision making and goal setting. The validity of such assessments rests upon how effectively the stakeholders negotiate assessment practices that draw upon shared communal guidelines while providing opportunities for individual creativity.

In terms of notions of reliability, we see assessments as verifiable and grounded in examinations of the artifacts of learning and decision making, which is more suggestive, useful, and interpretative rather than definitive, abstract, or requiring agreement (see Moss, 1996, in press; Moss & Schutz, 2001). We see notions of consistency and consensus taking a back seat to explorations and entertaining multi-perspectives as one considers various solutions and different pathways. Our view of assessment includes:

- Teachers having a fuller sense (expanded, refined, different) of the students' abilities, needs, and instructional possibilities;

- Students having a fuller sense of their own abilities, needs, and instructional possibilities;

- Teachers integrating assessment with teaching and learning (this would entail the dynamic, ongoing use of assessment practices, as well as assessment tailored to classroom life); accommodating, adapting, adjusting, customizing—shifting assessment practices to fit with students and their learning and adjusting teaching in accordance with feedback from assessments;

- Students engaging in their own self-assessments as they set, pursue and monitor their own goals for learning in collaboration with others, including peers, teachers, and caregivers.

- Communities of teachers, students, and parents forming and supporting one another around this assessment process.

We see teachers, students, and caregivers operating in a kind of public sphere where they are part of the team (as the teachers, students, and community work together developing and implementing curriculum plans or ponder the right questions to ask to spur students' reflections, develop insights, and learn). In many ways teaching involves continuous experimentation and adjustments to plans, directions and future goals. "Teachers have to be a mix of ecologist, developer, advocate, coach, player, actor-director, stage manager, mayor, and sometimes counselor as they develop and implement plans recognizing the need make constant adjustments to what they are doing and what they might have expected to do next" (Tierney, 1997). Mike Rose (1995) suggests in *Possible Lives* that classrooms are created spaces, and the ones that are successful are those that create spaces where students feel safe and secure; they are the classrooms in which students pursue their interpretative authority for themselves and with others. In a similar vein, Kris Guiterriz et al. (1995), asserts the need for spaces where we can connect or transact with each other, rather than pass by one another.

Tradeoffs in Pursuing the Described Types of Assessment Partnerships

For some, negotiating such changes is not easy. It involves risk taking, a willingness to experiment, and an ability to persevere when at times the visible rewards are not quickly realized. However, we see the value of these partnerships as far outweighing the negative aspects. An assessment partnership approach requires time to plan and implement. It means that easy, quick assessments of the complexities of learning will not suffice. We see a need for a willingness to embrace a spirit of progressive refinement by all of those invested in assessment partnerships. This spirit necessitates that teachers be flexible and willing to have ongoing conversations with stakeholders regarding assessment and be willing to revise their practices as a result of these conversations.

However, we see an increased interaction among students, teachers, parents, and other stakeholders as these assessment partnerships are developed, enacted, and refined. We believe this approach closely links teaching, learning, and assessment in both philosophical and practical ways. A partnership approach creates ways to cultivate a culture of assessment anchored in what learners are actually doing, not what they cannot do, and thus move beyond a deficit model toward a more constructivist, inclusive, and, we believe, interactive view of the evaluation of learning.

In these next chapters, we discuss the rationale and process that inform and support interactive assessment partnerships in more detail and then delineate specific approaches directed toward developing partnerships. We believe this way of rethinking and developing assessments with stakeholders will move assessment to a space where it will help teachers, parents, and especially students pursue a type of assessment that is proactive and developmental while facilitating achievement and learning.

Four

Negotiating Partnership Through Interactive Assessments

In this chapter, we take a closer look behind the scenes at the negotiations and considerations that underpin partnership, as well as at steps that can be taken to achieve teachers', students', and parents' goals.

The Basis for Negotiation

All interested parties need to be represented in negotiations. They are all involved in sharing information and making decisions together. This is a team approach in that decisions are made together, based on recommendations by all interested parties.

The teacher is responsible for pulling together the team and developing the format for the negotiation, with consideration being given to the best venue and the ground rules to be followed. As will be seen in Part III of this book, Assessment Conversations, these conversations may take the form of student-led conferences or parent-teacher conferences of various types. Whatever format the teacher selects, the primary goal is to allow all interested parties to have a voice in the negotiations, particularly in the setting of educational goals for students.

Steps to Assessment Partnership and Interactive Decision Making

There are a number of steps that underpin decision making, as outlined below.

◊   Gathering the Resources

  •   Students, teachers, and parents gather relevant material prior to meeting.

◊   Reviewing the Material

  •   Teacher and students conduct classroom-based review of student work in preparation for reports to parents, parent-teacher conferences, or parent-student conferences.

  •   Student researches efforts and achievements toward organizing a tour involving discussion of goals, progress, features, achievements, and future goals. This might occur in conjunction with conferences or open houses or via reports to be shared.

  •   Teacher reviews student efforts and achievements.

  •   Parents review student efforts and achievements.

  •   Teacher discusses features, achievements, and progress to date.

◊   Setting Goals and Planning to Meet Future Needs

  •   Students, teacher, and parents discuss concerns and suggestions.

  •   Students, teacher, and parents plan ways to meet the student's needs.

  •   Students, teacher, and parents plan for ways of checking on progress toward goals.

◊   Conducting Ongoing Reviews

  •   Teacher evaluates the process and devises ways to improve the student and parent review, assessment, and goal setting.

  •   Other teachers review material to gauge quality and provide feedback on procedures, criteria, and other areas.

Gathering the Resources

A host of material can and should be available to the teacher, students, and parents as they review what students have been doing and make plans for next steps. Such materials could include portfolios, dossiers, other class work, observations, and material from outside school. We think that better and more informed decisions will emanate from multiple sources. Making decisions depends upon an ability to be informed about what students do over time rather than any reliance on just scores on quizzes. To this end, we recommend that the teacher maintain an ongoing file of class work, rough drafts, planning notes, journals, finished products, and photographs. See Part II of this book, Assessment Artifacts, for more information.

In Barbara's classroom, when conference time nears there are stacks of the students' material on a table at the back of the room. The students also have access to a file cabinet where they organize their ongoing portfolios as well as past portfolio material. As Barbara prepares for teacher-parent conferences she meets with her students at the back table. Together they look through their work from among the stacks. In turn, they review and discuss their progress, consider needs to be met and recommendations for change, and formulate what might be shared with the parents.

Reviewing the Material

Conversations With the Student as Tour Guide and Researcher

Conversations are usually the means by which the review of material occurs, with all parties discussing efforts and achievements reflected in the assessment artifacts. The conversation might occur in the context of an open house or conference. In some cases, the conversation around a student's portfolio might occur at home. Following are some examples of how materials are reviewed and selected.

Example 1: Suzanne's Class

Suzanne is in the ninth grade. In Suzanne's classroom, she and her classmates gather material from various units and projects completed over the past month. The teacher asks them to look over their efforts and to suggest features that they noticed about their work. A brainstormed list of these features is developed and then used by the students to generate different rubrics for themselves to judge their own work. These rubrics are added to their folders and serve as a basis for conversations with their classmates and their teachers about their work. The teachers also use the rubrics as part of the conference with the parents and include them with their own assessment of the students' work that they send home to the parents.

Example 2: Christopher's Class

In Christopher's first-grade classroom, the teacher also brainstormed with the students a list of features that each child was to find from the material that they had gathered. Christopher's teacher had him look over his reading log and to check two or three books that he enjoyed as well as books that he found easy and others that he found more difficult. From their portfolios, students were to select three different pieces that they had written and liked. They were to write why they liked their pieces and to choose one that showed improvements. The teacher also asked the students to compile story problems that they did for mathematics as well as material from science experiments and other class projects. Together the students and teacher made a list that was to serve as the agenda for what the students would share at the student-parent conference and open house or a sharing meeting at home. The teacher wrote a note to the parents to explain the procedure and provide guidelines for the parents' responses.

In both classrooms, the teacher orchestrates the review but the assessment and selection of the work is done by the students. In addition, students organize the material for the conference as well as provide comments on their own work. That is, the review of the material by the teacher and parents is under the direction of the student, whether or not the student is present at the conference. The student is a tour guide to the world of his or her work and thinking. It is important to have the student walk parents and teachers through what they did, what they liked, and what they learned, as well as some of the things with which they may have struggled.

Generally, there is a sense of celebration as one learns about the student's work. In pursuing the tour, we think that it is important that we avoid an overly global pronouncement or anything negative, but instead embrace the complexity and individual character of a student. Where there are problems in learning such as a lack of motivation to learn or difficulties with the material, there are times and places for conversations about those problems. For example, the teacher and the parents may opt to hold a meeting to discuss these things. Other possibilities for problem solving are discussed in chapter 10. The starting point of the tour of the student's work, however, should be a positive one in which all participants find and discuss what the student can do.

The primary role of the parent and teacher is to support the student, and as such, they need to listen and build upon the student's efforts, including helping the student access resources and refine decision making. In this role, we encourage the teacher and parent to compliment the student by finding specific things that are honestly good about the student's work rather than rejecting or reacting negatively to their efforts.

In the early 1990s, when the notions of student self-assessment began to emerge, many of us viewed it as an activity that one did to students rather than with them. While we recognized that a primary goal of assessment should be student assessment or student decision making, our approach was limited—a worksheet or self-assessment checklist to be completed or a rubric that was filled out.

Now we tend to see self-assessment as a process involving decision making, which students learn to do with increasing sophistication as they become adept at using different evidence, different lenses, different perspectives, and moving ahead on the possibilities.

Having concrete evidence or observations are key elements. These might include charts, webs, lists, plans, sketches, rough drafts, photographs or videos of students engaged in learning, or simply recounting what one planned, how one proceeded, and what one achieved. As students proceed they have countless opportunities to see themselves—their plans and goals as well as the strategies they use and the outcomes and products that they achieve. Metaphorically speaking, what teachers need is a combination of some form of video replay, mind probe, mirror, and time lapse machine, in order to recycle the work that is done instead of disposing of it.

The decision making involved in gathering these collections can begin with the start of any new unit, project, or topic. A teacher might have students begin a unit with material that they have already completed on the topic and begin to map, web, or chart what they already know and might be interested in exploring. By having students develop such charts, either individually or as a group, they can discern unanswered questions and areas for further exploration while developing plans for what they might pursue. As they proceed they can extend the chart or add to the web, monitoring their progress in an ongoing fashion. The material that they gather can serve as a working folder of source material.

Teachers as Assessors

Sometimes the most effective classrooms seem to operate themselves, but usually there is a teacher who has organized the classroom to ensure success. Behind the scenes of partnering and interactive assessment practices, the teacher plays a key role not only in guiding students but in gathering and monitoring student goal setting, learning processes, problem solving, and achievements. In other words, teachers are involved in their own ongoing observations and record keeping as they engage with their

Some Thought on Student Self Assessment

The primary goal is to expand the assumptions that students use to assess themselves and make decisions. Students should reflect upon what they have done with an eye to what they might do next. Thinking about assessment, therefore, should be integrated with considering goals. Assessment is a recursive process of ongoing negotiation with partners for the purpose of pursuing ongoing development

One of our primary goals is to help students make decisions that are useful toward achieving next steps, at the same time as we expand the repertoire of strategies (such as evidence or criteria) that they use to judge themselves in terms of process, product, and action plans. Ideally, teachers might develop their own ever changing "to do" list with the students and the parents, but to spur thinking we have devised our own list.

Reflecting and Deciding on Next Steps

- Focus on the goals—ask students to discuss what their goals are and how they decided to pursue them. Be aware that sometimes student goals (which may be clear versus poorly defined, too specific or overly general, among other things) may be key to understanding the path they followed and the outcomes that were produced.

- Consider process and product, strategies and outcomes.

- Probe versus telling students. Remember, the goals is to have the

cont.

students doing the same. On a day-to-day basis as well as weekly or monthly, teachers and students are engaged in a cycle of activity that involves observational checks, reflections, consultations, and joint decision making. Figure 4-1 shows how such a cycle might look.

As they proceed through the cycle, teachers use various guides to help in decision making. Some are based upon the difficulty level of the material. For example, literacy teachers will often use oral reading accuracy or the informal reading inventory to assess the students' reading level. Some will benchmark the students' performance using test items or samples of writing quality devised by state or national standards.

cont.

students assess themselves rather than have you assess them.

- Follow the student's lead.
- Respect their criteria for judging their work. Avoid overly preset criteria.
- Help them see what they have done that has been effective rather than what they see as weaknesses. Some students may focus on the negative rather than the positive.
- Have students show you rather than just talk about what they have done.
- Encourage students to share their efforts and criteria with others.
- Emphasize and encourage individual differences. Avoid ranking students.
- Have students develop their own criteria in a menu-like fashion, perhaps emerging from rubrics.
- Encourage students to "circle" their own work, i.e., looking at it from different perspectives.
- Start the conversations using a variety of means, describing their work in terms of metaphors or graphically.
- Listen to what others have done or are thinking about doing as a way of deciding what they might do.
- Incorporate assessment during the whole project process; avoid leaving it solely until the end.
- Pay attention to and draw attention to process, growth, and risk taking.

Figure 4-1. Cycle of Observational Checks, Reflections, and Decision Making.

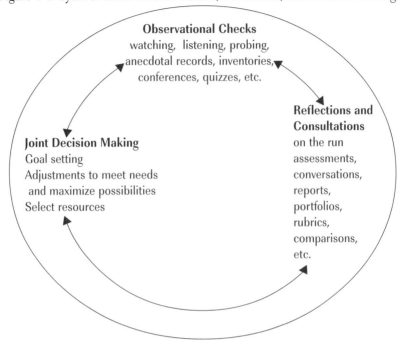

Periodically a teacher will use a summary guide to keep tabs on progress, as a resource for conferences or as part of their ongoing record keeping. Summary sheets take various forms, but what is key is that the form should coincide with the goals of the classroom. Figure 4-2 is an example of a type that is often used.

Some teachers correlate these guides with the elements that they list on report cards; others use the guides as a basis for a narrative-style comment. In particular, the teacher might use the list as a guide to reflect upon the student's work and the teacher's own observations in discussing the student's progress. For instance, a teacher might offer comments such as the following:

> Xavier has been engaged in inquiry about the world around us. He has read a range of material, and, as you would expect, is beginning to enlist a range of appropriate strategies including when he reads material that he finds challenging. For example, I think that Xavier understood the details and plot but wrestled with reading the "Island of Blue Dolphins" especially in terms of visualizing possibilities and generating his own questions. But he was very resourceful and delved into reading about the ocean and islands as a way of thinking about the story and what was happening. He offered some wonderful reactions and interpretations when he was reading one of the science fiction books. He has read and followed a great deal of science fiction and uses his knowledge of different selections to make connections across them. If you look across time, he has pursued a lot of books for

enjoyment tied to his interests and is willing to delve into books with less familiar settings and to learn new things. Across time Xavier has been engaged in a range of books (let's look at the log) and they seem to be getting more challenging.

Some teachers will include in their review other information such as standardized test results. By themselves test scores may not reveal actual classroom performance and they certainly do not help students and parents know the next steps to take to improve. However, this information can be useful when included along with qualitative information (actual writing, self-evaluations, homework papers, and so forth) that are collected and reviewed.

Figure 4.2. Sample Summary Sheet

Name: Date:		Inde- pendent	Some Support	More Support	Not Observed
Engagement: **Thoughtfully/Actively** Comments: *Has reluctance* *to predict, set purposes,* *self-question. Likes to talk* *about experiences in his* *life. Tends to be hesitant* *to select book.*	Actively engages	☐	☐	☑	☐
	Sets own purposes	☐	☐	☑	☐
	Relates to self	☑	☐	☐	☐
	Relates to other texts	☐	☑	☐	☐
	Self-initiates	☐	☐	☑	☐
	Other: *Has rich back-* *ground that surfaces* *occasionally.*	☐	☑	☐	☐
Learning Strategies Comments: *Becomes* *personally involved with* *questions such as "If* *you . . ." Wonderful in* *terms of evaluating ideas.* *Tends to stop when* *confronting difficulties.*	Previews, questions, predicts	☐	☐	☑	☐
	Connects ideas	☑	☑	☐	☐
	Judges ideas	☐	☐	☐	☐
	Becomes personally involved	☐	☑	☐	☐
	Uses cueing systems & cross-checks	☐	☐	☑	☐
	Troubleshoots	☐	☐	☐	☑
	Keeps tabs & organizes	☐	☐	☑	☐
	Responds & reflects	☐	☑	☐	☐
	Other: *Appears to need* *encouragement to self-* *correct*	☐	☐	☐	☐
Collaborativeness Comments: *Enjoys working with* *friends and is a productive* *contributor giving input,* *sharing, taking advice, etc.*	Shares	☐	☑	☐	☐
	Works jointly	☐	☑	☐	☐
	Helps others	☐	☑	☐	☐
	Uses input from others	☐	☑	☑	☐
	Proceeds self-confidently	☐	☐	☐	☐
	Other:				

cont.

Understandings Comments: *Understands what is read, but does not go beyond text.* *Needs to connect reading to his writing.*	Develops overall understanding	☐	☑	☐	☐
	Achieves set purposes	☐	☑	☐	☐
	Understands:				
	Key ideas/main idea	☐	☑	☐	☐
	Sequence, plot, structure	☐	☑	☐	☐
	Details	☐	☑	☐	☐
	Setting	☐	☑	☐	☐
	Character	☐	☑	☐	☐
	Author's craft	☐	☐	☑	☐
	Explores possibilities	☐	☐	☑	☐
	Explores goals/themes	☐	☐	☐	☐
	Other:	☐	☐	☐	☐
Going Beyond & **Making Connections** Comments: *Reluctant to pursue other material but once started he is keen.*	Follows up	☐	☐	☑	☐
	Connects with other work	☐	☐	☑	☐
	Applies to real world	☐	☐	☑	☐
	Pursues interests in other material	☐	☑	☐	☐
	Locates other material	☐	☑	☐	☐
	Other:	☐	☐	☐	☐
Self-Assessment Comments: *Tends to want others to make decisions for him.*	Aware of strengths, needs	☐	☐	☑	☐
	Improvements/ achievement	☐	☐	☑	☐
	Sets learning goals	☐	☐	☑	☐
	Implements goals set	☐	☑	☑	☐
	Maintains logs, records, portfolio	☐	☑	☐	☐
	Other:	☐	☐	☐	☐

Parent Review of Student Work

As partners in the decision making, it is important for the parent to be involved in the child's ongoing learning experiences. Parental engagement in providing support for their child does not end at the school door nor does teacher's support of the students end as they leave the school. Engagement involves three-way exchanges between teacher, students, and parents. A goal of the assessment partnerships is to increase the quantity and enhance the nature of these exchanges.

Carol Neutzing is a high school teacher with whom we had an association as we initially explored portfolios. She was keen to have her high school students share their portfolios with their families. As she discussed possibilities with her students, one of them asked if he could bring things from home. She asked if he meant homework. He said, "No—things we work on at home!" While tentative and skeptical about the possibilities, she agreed that he could add things from home. Her skepticism turned to delight as students added a range of material including song lyrics, music they had written, letters that they had received, and magazine articles, among other things. She realized that she needed to redefine homework and how students, regardless of age, liked to share who they are and what they do. In turn, when students shared their portfolios, they were sharing more than just schoolwork; they shared things that mattered to them.

Visitors to the Regio Emilia Preschools in Italy find that parental involvement is markedly different from what many of them have encountered elsewhere. Parents and other community members are part of a team that remains informed or involved in the day-to-day functioning of schools. Often, the parents of children at the school will take visitors on a tour, offering information on the projects and activities and their significance. In some classrooms, teachers engage parents and the community in a manner that is ongoing and that directly supports student learning. Parents read to children, listen to them read, help the teacher with filing, or simply join the class for excursions. In some classrooms, students pursue projects for and with parents, such as putting together a flyer, or the parents will contribute resources or stories to support student explorations of different topics. Indeed, a hallmark of schools in some locations is the feeling that the schools involve the entire community.

Whether or not a school or teacher develops such a sense of community and the parents are consulted regularly, we encourage teachers to develop procedures to ensure that parents have an intimate knowledge of the classroom and their own child's progress and activities. We suggest teachers ensure that parents have an opportunity to review their child's activities and seek reciprocity in terms of having parents inform them of the student's out-of-school activities.

In the context of pursuing a fuller partnership, we advocate activities that afford parents the opportunity to review, provide input into decision making, and make plans as well as adjustments to support students. We encourage teachers to create opportunities for parents to periodically review their child's achievements and to explore with their child different lenses by which to examine their efforts and achievements. The teacher will want to contextualize the student's work in terms of the projects that the students are doing or the relationship of the student's work to classroom goals. While this may be apparent from the nature of the projects, a number of teachers and schools will send portfolios or report cards home with details of the units that they are pursuing across the subject areas.

It is important that parents support rather than judge the students' work. Teachers should guide the parents' review so that they understand the nature of what they have been asked to do (keeping in mind there are additional procedures outlined in chapter 10 of this book for students who need special support). In a grade 3 classroom, the teacher sent home portfolios for parent reactions without explaining the nature of the work or how parents might respond. While most parents embraced their children's work and praised their efforts, a couple of parents focused on the weaknesses—elements such as misspelling, untidy work, and grammar. The teacher regretted that she had not explained the context and been more explicit about the types of reactions that would be helpful. She called the parents and discussed what had occurred in preparation for subsequent sharing.

In the context of student-led conferencing, portfolio sharing, and report cards, we encourage teachers and parents to act cooperatively in support of the student rather than judgmentally. When negative situations arise (for example, a student-led conference at which a parent responds negatively and moves the discussion toward the student's weaknesses or responds to a report card in an overly negative fashion), we encourage teachers to adjust or to follow up the situation so that the course can be redirected.

The review process should involve assessing the partnership and initiating activities that build the relationship. To this end, teachers should look for ways to share student work with parents. They should also consider some of the lenses that might be used to look at student work. Chapter 5 discusses some lenses for benchmarking students, including checklists and observations. Key to the partnership is the building of trust and respect, including assurances of confidentiality.

Setting Goals and Planning to Meet Future Needs

In some ways, goal setting and planning to meet future needs may be viewed as the key steps in consummating an assessment partnership. Certainly, they represent steps from which parents are likely to have been excluded unless the school was dealing with exceptional circumstances. Student involvement, however, may be less rare with the advent of portfolios and the increased attention given to student self-assessment.

Student-led and parent-teacher conferences have become a venue at which decision making has occurred. The following is one teacher's description of her approach (Allington, Butler, & Tierney, 1993):

> My goal was a minimum of one teacher-student conference per grading period. I always worked toward two. Sometimes I had these conferences during class time. At other times we met after school so that a student would be able to talk freely about his or her work without disruptions or distractions. Some students preferred the after-school slot so that they could have more privacy. They were sharing things about their writing and reading that they didn't want anyone else to hear. I respected that. Others wanted the extra attention and time from me. I'd recommend that you avoid the hubbub of the classroom while holding conferences yet still manage to keep an eye on your class at the same time. Other

teachers I know accomplish his by using teacher aides and parents for conferencing. I found that one-on-one time I spent with my students so valuable in terms of gaining personal and instructional insights that I couldn't delegate the job to someone else.

My students came to the conference with something that they had read recently, their reading logs, writing logs, self-assessment forms, and port-folios with a recent selection of their writing. I came with my anecdotal records, assessment managers, and my ears. My role was primarily that of a listener. . . .

I asked them open-ended questions that also helped them set goals as follows:

- Tell me about your piece of writing/what are you reading?
- How did you come to write this piece/read this?
- What do you need help on?
- What do you want to develop further?
- What do you think are the high points of what you've done?
- How does this compare with what you've written/read earlier?
- Where will you go from here? What are your plans?

Students often have answers to their own questions or problems. We need to allow them time to reflect back on former times and experiences to see if they can come up with their own solutions. Only if the student probes and reflects and still has no ideas do I offer suggestions.

After a conference, the student would either take away a reaffirmation of the direction in which he or she was going or start on another path. I'd use what I'd learned from the conference to inform or redirect my lesson plans and guide students' own decision making. As a result of conferencing, I was often able to find mini-groups of students who were unsure about a strategy or an area of writing. I prepared mini-lessons for those students so that I no longer had to allow whole-class time-outs for something only a few students needed. (p. 30)

We suggest taking an approach to setting goals whereby students ex-plore what they know and may have done, along with reflecting on their interests and possible goals. It is akin to the notion suggested by Short, Harste, and Burke (1995) of "wandering and wondering" prior to mak-ing a commitment to specific areas of interest to be pursued. While goals can emerge as one completes an assignment, course of study, or project, goals seem best if they are developed at the inception of a project rather than at the end. At the beginning of the project (in conjunction with wan-dering and wondering), goals tend to reflect a proactive stance and are more concrete; at the completion of a project they seem somewhat more judgmental and summative. Also, they are often vague if they are not ongoing. The example below may serve as an illustration.

Simon's class often pursues projects. As Simon completes a project, he assesses himself. As he begins the next one, he sets goals that build upon what he has done in the past. For example, as Simon contemplated a project focused on pollution, he recalled a story about a movie he had seen (*Erin Brockovich*). He was aware that his family had decided to stop using tap water so he knew he had a basis for exploring some issues. He gathered material from magazines and old newspapers as well as books and web sites. He set some goals, some dealing with how he would research and develop the project, some with content, and others relating to how he would pull together the material. Some also related to people that he might work with—classmates, friends, family members, and others.

In setting goals, remind students to set at least three types of goals or plans:

- goals related to content or problems that they are interested in exploring

- goals related to the strategies they intend to use to investigate or to problem-solve, including locating and organizing resources

- goals related to troubleshooting, self-assessing, and obtaining feedback

In one classroom where we studied student-teacher and parent-teacher conferencing, we observed similar practices, but also ones that connected with the parent-teacher conference and report cards. An example follows:

The third-grade teacher would meet with each if her students for 10 to 15 minutes to go over their portfolios and other work and to share perspectives. The student-teacher conference preceded the parent-teacher conference. In preparation for their meeting, the teacher would discuss the report card as well as what the student might want to have the teacher share. The teacher asked each student the question "What would you like me to share with your parent?" Children took the question earnestly. In one instance, the child paused a long time before answering, but then looked at the teacher and said, "I know my Dad is concerned about my reading. Tell my Dad how well I am reading now and how I am getting better." The teacher asked if there were things he would want to show his father. The child suggested showing him some of the stories he had written and his responses.

These conversations between the teacher and students included queries by the teacher on how the teacher might help. The children took the question seriously and often suggested how the teacher might be able to respond better to the students' needs. For example, one girl suggested that she needed more time and sometimes wished the teacher could let her continue working on a project. The teacher and student discussed a way for the girl to signal the teacher when this was the case.

When conducting discussions with parents, teachers should share their perspectives and observations of the student and provide an opportunity for the parents to do the same. Of particular importance are any parental observations in the context of looking over what the student has done and in thinking about the future. Some of the more useful questions are:

- What would you like to see us continue to emphasize?

- How would you like us to emphasize them?

- Are there other things that you would see us emphasize and how?

- Do you have suggestions for how I might support your son and daughter better than I have?

- What types of things do you think that we could support together or you might support?

In discussing these queries, teachers should share their own and the student's opinions, as well as what is emphasized in the classroom and how students have been supported in their work. We have also found it important to discuss next steps (e.g., the next unit, workshop, or mini-lessons), including specifics of how to proceed in the context of the next set of assignments.

Conducting Ongoing Reviews

Just as any complex behavior takes constant refinement, experimentation, and exploration in different situations with different students and community members, partnerships in decision making require constant exploration and reflection. Sometimes it might require asking for input from others, perhaps a peer, a teacher, an outsider, or a group of interested parties. It might involve looking back or looking at different possibilities. Perhaps it suggests that learning to partner requires a willingness to experiment.

We suggest that there is a need to pursue an ongoing refinement of the assessment partnership in terms of the following:

- the concerns and needs of the various stakeholders

- the quality and dynamics of the partnership

- the quality of the decision making and support

- the features that are examined and viewed as signs of development

- the legal aspects, especially if there are high stakes involved

The Concerns and Needs of Stakeholders

The assessment system should include a review by parents, students, other teachers, and school personnel. It should include judgments of their satisfaction as well as how the assessment system contributed to their understanding, the quality of decision making, and support for student learning. For example, principals are apt to have the following concerns:

- that the procedure is well-developed and defensible

- that the curriculum goals are covered

- that it works across the grades

- that it integrates with other assessment activities

- that it develops an ongoing and productive relationship with parents

They want to understand the impact of the assessment approach, not just the parents' and students' satisfaction level but also the influence of decision making on subsequent success.

Many teachers are concerned with finding a good fit with their classroom goals as well as with manageability in terms of time and resources. For this reason, they will be concerned with how "workable" the assessment system is, including how flexible and demanding it will be to implement. For many teachers, it is important that the assessment partnership meets ongoing goals for their students and that it be easily integrated with what they already are doing. Timing the implementation and the dovetailing of the activities with other elements may be key. Teachers are sensitive to how the process might enrich student learning and to the level of support from parents. Their concerns contain elements such as the following:

- is dynamic and manageable

- can be accomplished in a reasonable time

- meets student needs

- meets parents' needs and strengthens the partnership

- encompasses ongoing classroom assessment and testing

- streamlines reports and record keeping

- fits with grading and comparisons

- encourages healthy working relationships between teachers and students, among the students themselves, and between the students and the parents

Resource teachers will also wish to be involved, and teachers need to ensure that the plans do not exclude them.

Parents vary in their concerns. Some will be excited about the possibilities their involvement will provide. Others will question what good it will serve their child, especially should there be any negative impact as their son or daughter progresses through the grades. Some will express allegiance to traditional grades, while others will express support for an approach that departs from grades as long as information about their child's growth is forthcoming. It is key that they acknowledge the worth of two major tenets of the partnership, namely, the importance of student engagement in self-assessment and the importance of their supportive role in helping the student learn. We also find that parents want adequate communication and some choice.

It is important to not underestimate the students' interests. Indeed, they have the major vested interest in the role of the new system. They will want to understand the purpose of what they will be doing and what the expectations of parents and others will be. As students move into adolescence they may wonder how genuine the approach is. They may also wish to interact with their parents around assessment matters in a manner that respects their maturity. They will want to be sure that their voices count. As one student suggested after she conferenced with her teacher and prepared to conference with her parents, "I feel as though I am not just being told, but I am also heard and can share things the teacher and my parents do not know."

Quality and Dynamics of the Partnership

The teacher and school personnel should review the processes as well as the nature of the interactions occurring across the partnership. In the medical profession, nurses and doctors maintain notes on how family members are supporting a patient, as well as on matters such as anxiety. We suggest that the teacher assess the assessment partnership in terms of the participants' roles, including examining ways that they can improve their engagement and understandings.

- Are different modes for sharing and reflecting upon progress offered?

- Do the ideas and suggestions of students and parents count?

- Have students (and parents) been provided ample time to explore their knowledge and interests and to engage in wondering prior to setting goals?

- Do students collect a range of evidence that they in turn revisit?

- Are students encouraged to take time out to assess themselves, consider their progress, and perhaps change or refine goals?

In terms of the partnerships and interactive assessments, the goal is to create a more open classroom and school in terms of who makes decisions and how they are made. As educators, we have been sensitized to issues such as who controls the floor and whether or not learners are initiating, expanding, or merely responding. We struggle to find venues where learners will have voice and where ideas beyond the teacher's have a place. Sometimes we find the best place for these discussions to be held is at a round table where we are involved in joint problem solving and where everyone's expertise is valued. Usually it occurs in an ongoing, pervasive fashion—via e-mails, notices, bulletin boards, listservs, threaded discussions, letters back and forth, conversations, open houses, conferences, and so on. In this book, we share some of the places and ways that we think partnerships might develop in the context of assessment and as an alternative to report cards. We are not just doing this so that we can say that we have a partnership, however. Our goal is to establish a space where relationships build and decision making occurs in a dynamic and increasingly powerful fashion.

Making Quality Decisions

We think that special attention should be given to looking at student development over time, especially the students' decision making.

- Are students supported in developing and expanding upon the criteria that they use to make decisions and assess their progress?

- When students judge themselves do they address plans, process, and progress as well as ongoing goals?

- Do you judge the quality of student and parent decision making (the evidence that is examined, the criteria used, and the plans made) versus the products?

Overall there should be an increase in quality of decision making as everyone learns more about interactive assessment and partnerships. There may be individual concerns to be addressed that affect the quality of decision making for individual students. Chapter 10 has suggestions for problem solving in order to improve quality.

Features as Signs of Development

Key to interactive assessment is the idea that there are many possible ways of assessing growth over time and that transactions between stakeholders involve revealing the logical connections between the artifacts and the idea of growth. A group of papers written by a student may not hold much meaning unless stakeholders have made an analysis of them, looking for shifts in the writing over time and thinking about what competencies those shifts represent. In Part II of this book, Assessment Artifacts, we further discuss several types of assessments and how they can represent and reveal development.

Legal Aspects

Assessment practices can have legal ramifications: positive ones, as in the rights afforded to parents of children with special needs; potentially neutral (or positive or negative depending on a number of factors), as in district, state, and federally mandated assessment practices; and negative ones, such as when biased assessment practices serve as gatekeepers.

As we point out in chapters 10 and 11, the practices we are proposing are congruent with laws regarding parental involvement in the assessment of children with disabilities. The practices in this book bring all parents into the assessment conversation in a significant fashion.

Obviously teachers must comply with legally mandated assessment practices; however, those practices need not preclude student and parent involvement in assessment and goal setting. If anything, the state becomes another participant in the conversation. Parents, students, and teachers can find many means by which students can meet mandated requirements and still incorporate students' own interests and learning styles in the process.

One other legal facet is the possibility of lawsuits by people who feel that children have somehow suffered as a result of assessment practices. It is important for teachers to be aware of laws that affect their classrooms and to ensure to the best of their ability that all classroom practices are fair, consistent, and not harmful. We discuss this further in chapter 11.

Friendly Audits

A key question that should underpin any assessment effort involves an assessment of oneself as teacher. This process, too, should involve a partnership. For example, at the Parker School in Massachusetts, a team of knowledgeable and experienced colleagues reviews the school's portfolios and the teachers' evaluations of these portfolios, considering expectations for students elsewhere. They do this to gauge themselves as well as to obtain recommendation for ways that they might better represent student progress. The use of critical friends to audit in this way seems an excellent example of how we might move beyond the simple minded and reductionistic use of test scores for comparisons.

Teachers in Vista High School in Colorado have developed a comprehensive approach that involves the student convening a committee of teachers, classmates, family members, and/or adult friends. The segment below describes the results.

> A student's education at New Vista is divided into two stages. In Stage I, students work with their advisors to develop Personal Plans based upon interest, curiosity, strengths, and weaknesses. Questions that focus plans include: "What is of interest to me? Where might I be going after high school? What are my goals now and in the future? What are my strengths and where do I need improvement? What do I need to learn?" This first stage of exploration leads to Stage 2 and the completion of a student's high school experience. Stage 2 has a greater focus and is supported by a graduation committee that, with the student and advisor, identify courses, community experiences, mentors, and other learning experiences that will benefit the student and help him or her to meet goals.

The graduation committee is a group of adults and students who are selected by the student to help design and implement a graduation proposal. This committee identifies what the student needs to accomplish and assesses the movement of the student toward graduation. It is the responsibility of the graduation committee to make the final recommendation. The graduation committee includes five or six members:

- The student's advisor
- A community expert who is knowledgeable about the individual student path the student is planning to pursue and can provide specific guidance for what someone on that path does and needs to know
- A student who is at a similar point and can provide support
- A significant adult in the student's life (relative, friend, or other) who knows the student well and is trusted as a support by the student
- A student at an earlier stage who can observe
- [optional] An "ad hoc" resource person (e.g., a teacher at New Vista, another community person or expert, or other adult).

As the sidebar implies, assessment should be grounded in what students do rather than in a grade or score one or more steps removed from actual performance. In essence judgments should be tied to the primary sources of information rather than secondary sources. The difference between primary and secondary sources is significant to historians. A primary source might be actual documents or artifacts created during the period of time in question—diaries, letters, deeds, birth records, census data, newspaper accounts, and so forth. Secondary sources are like hearsay evidence in a courtroom—they reflect on the historical period but they are only as good as the primary evidence on which they are based. They may be removed from the actual time— as an autobiography written late in life differs from a diary kept every day—meaning that their conclusions are subject to

Interactive assessment involves a partnership around the following:

- collecting evidence: students engaged in capturing and making visible what they think and do, plan and achieve
- using various lenses: students using different ways of looking at what they did and expanding the criteria that they might use to judge themselves
- making judgments: students learning to make judgments as to their progress and future needs
- planning next steps: students learning to make possible plans based upon these judgments, the possibilities that they might envision, and the resources that they might be able to assemble effectively
- refining the process in terms of the amount and quality of parent and student involvement, and the extent to which the approach is manageable and meets the needs of the various individuals

forgetfulness, wishful thinking, defensiveness, and other foibles of the human mind.

Within a classroom, a piece of student writing, a reading miscue analysis, or a mathematics worksheet that contains a student's process as well as the answer he or she worked out is a primary source of information, that is, what the student actually does. A multiple-choice answer on a reading comprehension test or a mathematics achievement test is a secondary source of information because it was completed under artificial conditions In addition, it is not clear whether the student got an answer right because of knowledge, luck, guessing, vague recognition, or simply eliminating a couple of obviously wrong answers.

Assessment is not an end unto itself but needs to be reconnected to decision making and invigorating classroom life. Portfolios, conferences, and other assessment tools need to be evaluated in terms of how they support negotiations around the student's ongoing learning and the quality of the decisions that are made.

In sum, the key to effective assessment is a partnership that engages in ongoing exploration of a learner's engagements with a variety of lenses using an expanding criteria to reflect upon these engagements for purposes of making some judgments and considering possible goals and plans for achieving these goals. We suggest that teachers decide how to pursue interactive assessment in partnership with others, based on certain key roles:

◊ Principals and Teachers

- Supporting a climate of engagement with parents and establishing an atmosphere of student engagement in decision making and inquiry
- Creating spaces for exploration by the various stakeholders on issues of learning, assessment, and evaluation of student performance and curriculum planning
- Demonstrating respect for perspectives
- Developing procedures that have integrity and are consistent with legal requirements for reporting and access
- Reviewing and refining interactive assessment practices

◊ Teachers, Students, and Parents Together

- Engaging in observations and reflections on progress, goals, achievements, and next steps
- Supporting conversations that examine multiple perspectives and sharing on learning
- Gathering evidence along with different ways of benchmarking progress

- Developing summaries, reports, and communications to support and record decision making and ongoing inquiry
- Discussing needs and providing support and resources for student learning
- Developing procedures for informing comparisons of students—intra-individual (or with oneself) and inter-individual (with others)
- Reviewing practices and procedures for various stakeholders pertaining to decision making about students

Assessment Schedules

Partnerships are pursued daily—if not in terms of direct conversation, then through management of the materials that form the basis of the partnership. From the outset students and parents are involved in a cycle of gathering material and thoughts, reviewing progress as directions are set and reset, and reflecting on progress in concert with reviewing goals. Depending upon the class schedule and other considerations, these ongoing activities are calibrated to the initiation and completion of class projects, pursued daily, weekly, or monthly. Daily reflection constitutes the essence of ongoing partnerships, while serving as a background to more periodic reviews during planned interactions with parents such as conferencing or reporting.

Daily, partnership is developed and supported at the same time as student growth and students' assessments of their own growth are monitored. In terms of students' self-monitoring, we recommend that teachers focus on a straightforward cycle of self-assessment, namely, that students reflect on their efforts using an expanding set of understandings of ways to look at their work while making judgments of their progress and setting new goals.

Develop Term or Trimonthly Plans

Term or trimonthly interactions serve as a "time out" when the various parties can step back, organize, and get together to review progress over time. These events make self-assessment more formal. In some classrooms, they involve teachers and students organizing and reviewing portfolios and other projects in conjunction with plans for sharing with parents either through open houses, parent-teacher conferences, or student-led conferences. In some classrooms, it is an opportunity to organize computer files and to update home pages. In other classes, it represents the opportunity to formulate joint plans or to develop reports and serves as a time for the teacher to update notes. In many schools, these periodic get togethers vary across the year. Some teachers will plan a parent-teacher conference for the end of the first and fourth term and a student-led conference for the second and third. The method of reporting also varies. Notes might be developed together with parents and students after one session. A narrative report might be developed after another.

Consistent with the day-to-day focus, the periodic "time out" also focuses on the partnership with parents and students, as well as on the students' development and self-assessments. A focus of the periodic review should be on long-term goals, for example, strategy development or overall learning over time.

An annual review, which might be a combination of critical friends, surveys, analyses of progress, and self-assessment, can be helpful. Schools should annually assess the partnership system using a combination of critical friends (including parents and teachers from other schools) and inquiry about the impact the partnership might be having on the students and their parents. In Laura's school, for example, they enlist teachers from similar schools to review their assessment practices including the procedures they use to gather student work and judge its quality. They use these sessions as a way of assessing the reliability of their judgments as well as how their efforts compare with others.

Throughout the year, other initiatives by which schools can become more partnership centered should be examined and tested. Initiatives can range from town meetings with parents and students to regular times in the school day for parents or teachers to participate in ongoing conversation. Other formats include community advisory groups and web sites or voice mail numbers through which parents and students can interact or access information. You may need to develop a corps of community liaisons who can help build bridges of cultural understanding or help with translation for families of non-native English speakers.

Parents and students should not be regarded as guests or tourists, but members of a school family where there is conversation, cooperation, and flexibility. Top-down approaches to goal setting do not work. No one—teachers, parents, or students—likes to be told what to do without having some kind of input.

At the same time, opportunities for input must be authentic. Worse than having no input are the times when one knows one's opinion will be ignored, particularly if it is contrary to that of the "powers that be." Dishonest requests for input are often met with apathy, leading the person doing the requesting to the false conclusion that while input was encouraged, no one provided any. Soliciting opinions from stakeholders in an honest fashion can be discomforting. It requires stifling one's own defensiveness to listen openly to people with different perspectives, who nonetheless open up new possibilities. In chapter 10, there is a summary of listening skills that can assist in communication with stakeholders.

Schools need to consider ways by which they can open their doors to communities and support the diverse families whose children they serve. In our view, relationships are not something that one can dictate nor can they be built by a single person without the cooperation of others. Any schedule might be followed religiously to no avail, unless there is also an attitude of openness and willingness to pursue interactive forms of assessment.

Finally, we need to find ways to represent and discuss students' work across several years. Assessment systems should not be viewed as self-contained either within a classroom or for a single year. Assessment plans across classrooms and years should work together in a manner that supports reflections on educational efforts across the whole school as well as ways to progress based on what has been accomplished.

Some Examples

Interactive forms of assessment can be pursued in different settings, including informal and more traditional curriculum from elementary school through high school, in a variety of ways. Indeed, we would expect teachers to explore diverse approaches to partnerships as they pursue their goals and refine what works for them and their students. At times, the same teachers may use different approaches to partnership with different students or even the same student across time.

As a way of introducing some of the possibilities regarding how to proceed, here are some examples that represent classrooms and schools in pursuit of interactive forms assessment, followed by a more detailed set of suggestions of the steps that might be followed in setting up such systems. While the settings may differ and the methods vary, they share similar steps and principles in the ongoing pursuit of partnerships.

Stan's Method

Stan, a teacher in Massachusetts, was interested in moving toward student-led conferences throughout the year in lieu of traditional report cards. He discussed the idea with his principal who agreed to the pursuit as long as Stan had the support of the parents to do so.

At an open house at the beginning of the year, Stan introduced the parents to his goal and then followed up with a memo. The memo also involved a form to be completed by the parents whereby they indicated their choice of either a report card or the student-led conference followed by notes of the meeting. Although the majority of parents indicated they were interested in the student-led conference, some indicated a strong desire to have in place the traditional report card. Stan decided that he would retain the report card for those parents at the same time that he moved ahead with student-led conferencing.

Stan's class was set up around units and projects that cut across many of the subject areas as well as some class time that was allocated for specific subject areas. His students (fourth and fifth graders) were expected to keep track of their goals whether they were working on a project or in any of the subject areas, as well as maintain a file of their efforts, including rough work. The students were expected to date their pages and maintain one or more expandable folders where they kept their efforts. Most of the work was stored at school for safekeeping but would be shared with parents in conjunction with the student-led conferences to be held twice a year.

From the start of the school year, Stan emphasized goal setting with the students. The students set long-term goals as well as goals specific to projects. The goals were in several areas, including strategies they were to improve upon as well as knowledge areas that they wanted to pursue. At the completion of each unit and at the end of the term they shared what they had achieved, including things that they accomplished that went beyond the goal setting.

The student-led conferences proved to be a natural extension of their goal setting. At a meeting with their parents at which their work was displayed, they shared their statements of goals and explained how they pursued their goals. At the parent-teacher conference and in conjunction with the notes that Stan shared, he reemphasized the goals at the same time that he disclosed his view of the students' goals and their attainments. Primarily, he focused on the parents' views of the students' attainments. When asked about test results, he always had a copy of sample items and emphasized that the test was under different conditions and often covered material differently.

Stan's Plan

- At the outset—Parents and students were introduced to what Stan was planning and were afforded the option of traditional report cards or parent-teacher-student conferences as a means of sharing information about student progress.

- Yearlong—Emphasis was given to student goal setting, particularly as they started new projects and also as they periodically assessed their accomplishments. Expandable folders were used to collect student work, and these materials were reviewed by students, the teacher, and the parents.

- Bi-weekly —Students organized their folders and looked over their progress on the goals that they set.

- Tri-monthly—Student-led conferences were held with the teacher participating as necessary.

- Semi-annually—Parent-teacher conferences were held. As several parents were Spanish speakers, Stan also had a translator along. At the end of the year, feedback from parents and students was obtained and plans developed for the next year.

Laura's Method

Laura spearheaded the development of partnerships in conjunction with a movement toward portfolios in her high school. In addition, she worked at building support for the notion that teachers should work as teams, especially when reporting achievement. For a number of years, each teacher had developed his or her own elaborate scoring schemes with points distributed in different ways for work completed in the class. Laura spearheaded a more coordinated effort that involved a combination of parent-teacher conferences with student input along with an extended method of reporting based on audited teacher assessments of performance adequacy compared to age-related benchmarks. It sounds complicated but is rather streamlined.

Laura's Plan

- At the outset—Parents were invited to do a walkabout where they came to their child's school and followed his or her schedule. In each class, the teacher shared his or her goals on how he or she planned to engage the students in their various courses of study, including how the students would set goals together and keep tabs on their work and progress. Students were responsible for keeping a portfolio for each course of study.

- Yearlong—The teacher emphasizes that the students set goals and examine their attainments in conjunction with compiling portfolios. Separate projects, quizzes, and other assignments may be evaluated by the teacher, the students, and at times, peers. Each student also has an advisor who monitors the student's progress and acts as a "point person" for the student, the team of teachers, and the parents.

- Tri-monthly—Students and teacher each develop a set of narratives or notes that describe what they did and what they accomplished. The number of narratives or notes usually corresponds to the number of courses of study pursued. Each narrative includes details of the projects and assignments done in class, the goals that the student pursued, and his or her attainments—that is, what he or she learned or completed and the effectiveness of the strategies employed. The narratives are shared with parents, who are invited to comment.

- Semi-annually—A parent-teacher conference is arranged so that the teacher and parent may look over the narratives and notes as well as the students' folders. On the night of the conferences, a series of 10-minute meetings are held with the parents, the student's advisor, and teachers. They discuss the future goals and needs and provide one another with input and suggestions.

- Annually—The teacher compiles a summary report that includes an overview of the student and a discussion, based on input from both student and teacher, of how the student has fared. The teacher team discusses each student's work against what they deem to be expected performance for a student of that age. As a check on the teachers' assessments of the student's performance, the school invites some colleagues from other high schools to assess a sample of their student work and to give feedback on their assessment. These assessments serve somewhat like an audit of the school's assessment system. The school's assessment processes and standards are discussed in an annual report that is distributed to the state education department.

Looking Across our Examples

Stan and Laura have adopted similar processes of collaborative involvement in students' learning to assess themselves. Theirs is a kind of partnered inquiry where students, teachers, and parents set goals as students learn, examine their accomplishments, and set goals through portfolios or other means of reflecting upon their efforts. These teachers used a combination of assessment approaches—parent-teacher conferences, student-led conferences, and narratives, among others. What is also noticeable is the extent to which they engaged parents and students in decision making from the outset. Whereas in some school settings, report card time is a once- or twice-yearly activity, partnerships integrate report cards with ongoing activities in classrooms across the year.

One should not assume that Stan, Laura, and other teachers do not encounter difficulties with implementing partnerships. They are constantly making adjustments in what they do, and this may vary across students and parents. They are aware that they need to support students in the context of the partnership as well as in the activities that are integral to the partnership (such as maintaining portfolios or reflecting upon work). At times, they have found themselves having to engage with a student's parents by telephone rather than face-to-face or to look for other opportunities of communicating with parents.

What Laura, Stan, and others are doing does not happen overnight; it takes some planning and refinement over several years. Yet, in many ways, it extends goals and activities that already exist in these settings. For example, Stan and the teachers at Laura's school were keen to have parents involved and had pursued a range of activities whereby students would assume some ownership of their own learning.

Some Concluding Remarks

While partnerships may be pursued in different settings in different ways, the notion of a partnership may support a shift in orientation as to how schooling should be approached in all facets—including assessment, day-to-day teaching and learning, and curriculum development. At the heart of our views is the value of interactive learning and the idea that the student should be learning to assess progress, set goals, and gather the strategies and resources to achieve them. Students should be partners in decision making as they learn to do these things for themselves. Whether the student is doing a project, engaged in problem solving, or participating in various forms of discoveries, enjoyment, or communication, the student or learner is engaged in learning, learning to learn, reflecting, and planning.

But to make such moves may entail building greater trust between schools, students, and their families. We hope that the suggestions and possible steps that we outline will contribute to building a foundation of trust that better supports student development and decision making that is transactional and judicious.

In so doing, we hope to develop an assessment system aligned to the following principles:

- Assessment should be viewed as a teaching and learning goal rather than solely as a matter of judging performance.

- Assessment should be viewed as ongoing and subject to change over time as needs and curriculum shift.

- Assessment should be based upon multiple measures.

- Classroom-based assessments and other, more direct observations should inform decision making.

- The goals of assessment may be the same, but there may be differences in the kinds of information that are gathered and ways that teachers, students, and parents assess.

- Assessment should include process and product, progress and achievement.

- A variety of means should be used to review, reflect, and report on decision making about student progress within the year (summaries and periodic conferences with parents, students).

- There should be ongoing refinement of the assessment system, including issues of manageability.

- Labels and scores need to be related to concrete examples of student work or observations.

- Parents should be engaged in their child's learning and help decide upon goals and learning opportunities.

- Students should be assessing themselves and engaging with their parents and teachers in joint review and decision making.

- Differences of interpretation should be respected and discussed.

- Resource personnel and other school personnel should be able to review and contribute to the assessment system and decision making within a classroom and school.

- The assessment system should be evaluated periodically to help refine procedures. The evaluation should include a review by parents, students, other teachers, and school personnel. It should encompass judgments of their satisfaction as well as how the assessment system contributed to their understanding of the student, the quality of decision making, and the support provided for student learning.

In the next section of this book we discuss assessment artifacts—teacher- and student-developed collections and summaries of student work. The systematic collection of materials along with a thoughtful approach to considering the meaning of these materials forms the basis for the partnership. Chapter 6, The Report Dossier, considers how teachers, students, and parents might communicate with one another about the artifacts. Chapter 7 introduces the use of digital assessments.

Part II

Assessment Artifacts

Five

Narrative Reports

Introduction

Teachers use narrative reports as part of classroom instruction on a regular basis. They might use narrative reports as a way to introduce a new work of literature, share information about activities or events, tell a story to illustrate something that students are learning about in a unit, or share information with parents or other caregivers about a child's progress or achievement.

The use of narratives is not new to the classroom. What may be new for some teachers, students, and parents is the systematic employment of narratives as a way to more richly assess the type of learning that is taking place in classrooms. Narratives offer ways for teachers to individualize assessment while simultaneously informing parents about how a child is progressing in a detailed fashion.

In this chapter, we explore ways to conceptualize and implement narratives as a possibility for assessing learning. Then we provide some examples and templates for teachers to use in their classrooms in partnership with students and parents or other caregivers. As with previous chapters, we are not offering recipes; instead we are describing possibilities for teachers to develop a partnership with students and parents that fits with the needs and goals of their classrooms, schools, and communities. Consider the following exchange from a conversation that took place with teachers who were developing narratives as a feature of their assessment practices:

Cynthia: Why did you change from traditional report cards to narratives?

Teacher 1:   Our traditional report card was a checklist. It did not fit our
              needs. We had all of this information compiled from obser-
              vations. We wanted to tell our parents more about their chil-
              dren and what was going on in our classrooms.

Teacher 2:   Wouldn't you say that the traditional report card compared
              the child to a fictitious student at that grade level? Although
              it [traditional report card] was designed to look at each indi-
              vidual, it compared the child to an artificial standard. This is
              contrary to our philosophy.

Teacher 3:   With the traditional card, the "+," "-," and "N" were mythi-
              cally converted to A, B, and Cs. We take students where they
              are and move them forward. If a parent did not see all pluses,
              they were concerned, but that was not the case. So, the check-
              list format was totally against what we were trying to do.

It is evident from the responses above that these teachers were frustrated with the traditional reporting system that they were using. The
checklist format did not fit their curriculum or address the learning styles
of their student population. Their reporting system insufficiently described what was occurring in the classroom. These teachers sought alternatives in an attempt to communicate the child's progress more
accurately. The narrative format surfaced as a possibility and was adopted as a pilot study at this particular site. During that initial year, the teachers worked collaboratively with others across the district and met
frequently to debrief and to find ways to support each other during the
change process.

During visits to various other sites, we found teachers sharing similar experiences and thoughts. For example, Kathy, a third-grade teacher,
discussed her frustrations with the checklist:

> I found myself just checking off the boxes and not really focusing on the
> child's true development. Sometimes there was not a space to address
> the child's greatest areas of growth and strength. We are learning won-
> derful and exciting things and the [traditional] report card just did not
> do justice to what was going on in my classroom. I was ready to try
> something else. I felt very frustrated trying to make the report card fit
> the curriculum.

The above examples reinforce the notion that these teachers view assessment as a way to begin conversations about student learning. They
also exemplify ways teachers have encouraged and welcomed change
that supports input from both students and parents.

Building a Relationship

Building a relationship with parents and students is key when implementing student-centered assessment. One way teachers can involve
students and parents in the assessment process is to encourage and sus-

tain ongoing dialogue. Narrative reports can encourage and nurture this dialogue.

Incorporating narrative reports is not the only means of exchanging ideas. The teacher's narrative represents the ongoing management of the student and the parent in reflecting on the child's progress and the setting of goals. The teacher invites the parents and students to work together using the narrative report as a conversation starter for goal setting and planning, rather than as a summative and definitive statement. We encourage teachers to invite parents to follow up with thoughts and reflections about the information shared in the narrative. Remember, the narrative is not an end unto itself, but another way of supporting partnerships.

Developing the Narrative Report

The narrative report represents the teacher's desire to represent an individual student's goals, interests, and achievements. In order to encapsulate learning over time, some teachers involve students in this process through goal setting, which is then incorporated into the narrative. For example, one fifth-grade teacher shared how she incorporated information about her students into her narrative:

> Most of the activities in our classroom are open ended. The children are encouraged to make choices. I provide the raw materials and the children breathe life into the project. The narrative report gives me the opportunity to focus on how an individual responded to the unit of study. When you sit down with a blank sheet of paper, you have to focus on each student. Before writing the narrative, observations need to be recorded. I pay very close attention. I listen, watch, and record everything. Then, when I begin writing, I put everything on the table—a large table. Carefully, I go through the child's work samples so that I can communicate the child's progress as accurately as possible. A narrative links instruction and learning and tailors it to the individual.

Another elementary teacher, Tricia, discussed her approach:

> To write a narrative requires extensive knowledge of each child. There is only a blank sheet of paper. One has to rely on notes, observations, journals, and all the information gathered during that time period. By hyperfocusing, I am able to communicate to parents and the child with benchmarks their child has achieved. It really focuses me [on the student and forces me] to know my students.

The comments above indicate that narratives describe to parents what is being taught in the classroom as well as the individual student's progress.

Before writing the narrative, teachers need to develop a system for collecting, recording, and documenting learning and growth. Evidence of student growth and learning can be in the form of anecdotal notes (taken from classroom observations, individual conferences, or during

individual, small-, or large-group lessons), work samples (taken from journals and portfolios), and self-reflection forms. The teachers we interviewed
commented that the key to writing successful narratives is collecting evidence of each child's progress. Without this documentation, the teacher
is unable to pinpoint specific strengths and weaknesses. A narrative gives
the teacher an opportunity to illustrate rather than merely label how the
child is progressing. Written in a letter or story form, the teacher can share
examples of how the child engaged in various learning situations.

How and where the documents are stored differ by teacher. Some
teachers we interviewed kept binders with individual tabs for each student. Others mentioned they used portfolios that were marked for each
grading period, while a few created individual files on the computer that
housed work samples, anecdotal records, and observational notes. Regardless of how one stores the evidence, it is important that all materials
and documents are dated. This helps when the teacher or student critically examines the evidence and looks for patterns of learning and growth
over time.

How one writes a narrative is an individual choice. A critical first
step in writing the narrative is the organizational or coding system of the
information gathered. It is important that teachers select a particular system that enables them to identify progress and patterns of learning. We
found that many primary teachers (grades K–2) chose to organize their
materials through a thematic approach, whereas several higher grade
teachers (3–5) chose to separate materials by subject matter.

No matter how they organize the materials, many teachers follow a
similar format when writing the narrative. This format includes an opening paragraph, the body of the narrative, and the closing. The opening
paragraph usually describes the curriculum unit of study. Within this paragraph, some teachers may choose to describe the curriculum through the
daily classroom routine or provide a brief description of the course of study.
The body of the narrative typically includes information about the curriculum that the child is learning. It is within this section that the teacher will
describe the child's strengths and weakness in relation to the curriculum
content and the progress toward established goals. It is important to identify specific goals for further learning. Teachers may want to embed information describing work habits, social skills, and effort, as well as ways
parents can support this learning at home in the concluding paragraphs.
To close the narrative, teachers will want to describe their curricular goals
and make a brief summative comment about the child's overall progress.

When reviewing several narrative reports, we found that teachers frequently organized their narratives around two different formats: subject-
by-subject and thematic units. Examples of the types of narratives we
noticed during our site visits included total narratives written in story-
like or letter format, narratives that describe thematic unit teaching, and
checklists with short narrative—that is, a traditional report card with a

narrative as a supplement. The following are examples of the narrative types we have seen in use.

Example 5-1: Narrative in the Form of a Letter

Dear parents,

I wanted to have an opportunity to share with you some details of the last semester and Julie's progress and achievement.

As you may be aware, we are just bringing to an end the four units dealing with the needs of community and how communities work. The students were involved in reading several selections that dealt with children living in a variety of their neighborhoods. The focus of our discussion was how people lived together and how the setting impacted what they did. In conjunction with these units, the students explored the various services provided within a city and how decisions regarding the needs of a community are addressed. You might recall the field trip and how students were introduced to the city mayor's office as well as various services (medical, fire, water, etc.). The students were encouraged to interview different people who provided services to the city. In conjunction with our work in technology, students were given an opportunity to engage in a virtual tour of Harlem in the 1930s as well as to develop their own city with software. They were also expected to explore ways that they might enhance the city and to write reports and letters to support their efforts. As we explored these units, we attempted to relate their story problems in mathematics to this theme as well as to engage in some scientific problem solving related to the needs of cities (water flow, electric wiring, etc.). Likewise, spelling followed from what was accomplished in the unit. In conjunction with the spelling, Julie was encouraged to use these words in her reports. If you look through her portfolio, you will find examples of her exploration including some of the aforementioned efforts.

Julie did a variety of activities, as she was involved in these explorations. As she began this unit, she specified an interest in the following areas: understanding how a community works, capturing a better understanding of the five principles of government, and learning how individuals who work within a community fit within each of the principles. She established the following goals: (a) learn more about my community by researching one principle of government and sharing the information with others, (b) become a better speaker by working on my presentation style and performance, and (c) further my understanding and skills with technology by preparing and presenting my research project using PowerPoint, Inspiration, or KidPix software.

Julie was engaged in the planning, exploration, and development of various sets of materials. She is looking forward to sharing these materials with you during our research celebrations to occur later this month. You may have seen some of the materials, but you might wish to review them again with her as you review her portfolio that she'll be bringing home within the next couple of weeks. Be sure to listen to what she was trying to do and what she learned. In some cases, she achieved her goals—at other times, the goals changed. Also, remember that many of these pieces were under construction, so spelling and neatness may not have been stressed.

Julie did a superb job when locating both primary and secondary materials for her research project. She also worked diligently on creating the initial drafts of her illustrations and slides for her final presentation. She also sought assistance from the technology students in the school's computer lab as she pulled together her final project.

---

cont.

In terms of traditional social studies skills, Julie researched a variety of materials and developed an interview using a range of questions related to her interests and what she was trying to learn. Her questionnaire is included in her final project as well as in her portfolio. As you review her questionnaire, you may want to ask her to describe the process she followed as well as the type of responses she received when collecting the completed questionnaires. In conjunction with this activity, she was able to develop an understanding of important concepts such as cause-and-effect relationships. In her reading, she was independent in terms of locating material on the various topics and completing reading assigned in class. She responded very thoughtfully to her reading of several books that she selected for sustained silent reading. When she wrestled with a portion of the text, she understood her difficulty and used strategies such as rereading, thinking about what she was reading, or checking with others.

When I assessed how well she was handling the material, she read certain portions aloud and gave me a retelling. Her retelling was substantial and reflected her use of her own questions along with prior knowledge. Her reading reflected an understanding of key ideas and their interconnection. She was hesitant and needed support and encouragement to go beyond the text with possible interpretations. My checks on her oral reading indicated that she was able to read with very few deviations from the text that would impact her meaning making. Indeed, she demonstrated the ability to read these texts with little need for outside support. When children's oral reading is seen as frustrating the child and negatively impacting meaning making, we tend to shift to less challenging material. Julie seems to handle the material and I would expect could handle even more difficult text. She uses a variety of cueing systems (phonics, semantic or meaning, and syntax or grammar) very effectively.

Her writing reflected effective use of ideas from what she read in conjunction with using her own interests to shape what she pursues. She demonstrated an understanding of being able to make a point of support with details as well as how to formulate a letter asking for information. She carefully plans beforehand and as she writes and thoughtfully weaves together ideas using an understanding of story structure and report structure to organize the material. Also, she uses peer feedback and her additional reading to improve her work. When she revises, she adds ideas and changes her ideas to make the text more interesting. I am very encouraged with her expansions of her work in these ways, as many times revisions tend to be just spelling and grammar changes.

In mathematics, her reasoning reflected that she was capable of dealing with story problems involving comparisons of proportions. At times, she had to be prompted to relate what she was doing to her own experiences.

Her various creations (technology-based cities, reports, and artwork) represented an attempt to connect complex ideas thematically in a manner which reflected her interests. She seems to be developing a great sense of composition, an understanding of tools, and experimentation.

Her interactions with classmates are always positive. She is willing to work with different classmates and is an effective team member (making suggestions, providing support, making contributions, and willing to share). Her behavior in class and on the playground reflects an understanding of how to negotiate friendships with others and is very inclusive. While she likes competitive activities, she is quick to support all of her classmates.

Her portfolio represents a rich range of explorations and various other strengths. Please review the portfolio and let us know what you see as possible goals. Julie has reviewed her

cont.

portfolio for herself and has detailed her strengths and goals. She tends to be self-critical; but when probed, she recognizes what she has accomplished. Her goals tend to be emerging in ways which are concrete and tied to her background and interests. I am very pleased with the progress she is making, especially in the areas of technology, reading and comprehending informational books, and research and reference skills.

Thank you for the opportunity to share with you what we have been doing as well as the efforts of your child. I am so glad that we are able to work together on building a partnership to more fully support her development. Please don't hesitate to give me as much input as possible—especially related to some of the successes that you have noted and goals that you would like us to all consider especially as we plan ahead. E-mail me, contact me by phone, or simply write or come by. I look forward to hearing from you.

Thank you.

Sincerely,

P.S. Please add any feedback, insights or additional information that you like. If you would prefer that we also meet or that I call you, please let me know suitable times and a number to call.

Example 5-2: Narrative Describing Thematic Unit Teaching

Dear parents,

This report will describe the progress Kyle has made throughout this grading term. He is a delight to have in class. I have thoroughly enjoyed working with him and find his sense of humor and willingness to go the "extra mile" to assist a peer very refreshing.

Our learning this past semester was very inspirational and intriguing. We began our new unit on "Life Cycles" with an author study on Eric Carle. As we explored several books by Eric Carle, we asked the art teacher, Mrs. H., to assist us in learning about collage and to guide us through our own designs. Kyle, in particular, found this project to be very exciting. While working on his project, I noticed that he was very selective in the types of colors and shapes that he included. When he shared his completed project with the class, he was able to connect items in his collage with information he gleaned from several of Eric Carle's books we had read in class.

At the end of the author study, we had a class voting of our favorite Eric Carle book. I am pleased to report that *The Very Quiet Cricket* was the overwhelming choice of the students. I suspect that the sound of the cricket at the end of the book was a factor in this decision. We actually designed a classroom ballot that students were to complete in our "voting booth" during our language arts block. After the voting was complete, we counted the ballots and made a bar graph that illustrated the voting results. Kyle was selected as the "official recorder," and he was to complete the bar graph as the votes were tallied. This activity enabled us to learn how to develop and read bar graphs. Other math concepts that were reinforced during this author study were time (telling time and sequencing days of the week and months of the year). Kyle is beginning to grasp these concepts. He is able to recite the days of the week and months of the year. He has little difficulty with telling time to the hour, but needs to continue practicing telling time to the half hour. He is also able to identify the minute and second hands and count by fives to 60.

cont.

The Eric Carle author study also provided opportunities for the class to learn sequencing skills. Kyle had little difficulty identifying the events that occurred at the beginning, middle, and end of the story as he completed the caterpillar story map. He was very attentive and willing to participate as we completed the story map. When discussing the story and story map, Kyle was able to respond verbally using complete sentences and to identify the correct item and locate it correctly on the map,

When listening to each story read aloud, Kyle was an attentive listener and was a willing and excited participant in class discussions. He was able to identify events in the story and could successfully complete a retelling when asked. Kyle was also able to identify specific events from different stories by Eric Carle and could place information under the correct sections on a graphic organizer—we called this a story elements chart.

Our author study was a springboard to our work on the life cycle of insects in science. Grasping basic knowledge from the literature books invited further study we found in several nonfiction, informational books. Kyle thoroughly enjoyed completing his individual *K-W-L* chart. The questions he posed to the class on "What we want to know" were outstanding! These questions led to an in-depth discussion on several issues and it was decided that the class would complete a research project on a specific question. Kyle found this project to be both challenging and rewarding. He worked with a partner and was able to successfully demonstrate his understanding of finding information in reference books and to document this understanding on his data chart. As students worked in groups to complete their research, Kyle easily and willingly took on a leadership role in organizing the room so that it was conducive for study as well as collaboration. The research group to which he was assigned was a hard-working group that collaborated well together under his leadership. He was willing and able to assist others in locating information in several resources and led conversations and clarified information when needed. In the creation of the final project, Kyle encouraged the group members to experiment with technology by completing a presentation using the KidPix software. He truly guided and supported peer learning for those who were not as familiar or comfortable with this particular software. By the end of this project, the group members were satisfied and comfortable manipulating the program. The presentation was outstanding and the group's presentation ended with applause from the entire class. All presentations will be available for review during our spring open house that will take place later this month. I encourage you to ask Kyle to share this project with you. You will truly be amazed!

In closing, I would like to share that Kyle is truly a joy to have in class. I am impressed with his leadership skills, and his work habits and skills are to be commended. He has found much success this semester in all areas and is able to find connections in what he's learning. I would encourage Kyle to continue to read his literature book at home, and you can support him in this process by encouraging reading with him each day and providing time for discussions about what he's reading and learning at both school and home. I encourage and welcome your input and assistance in the classroom. Kyle will be bringing home his portfolio in the next few weeks. I encourage you to sit with him as he shares his work with you. He has purposefully selected many items that are "works in progress" that I think you'll find very interesting and engaging. I look forward to learning more about his plans for these pieces.

If you have specific questions or concerns on what we're doing at school, please do not hesitate to contact me via e-mail or call the school to discuss things with me or to schedule a conference. I look forward to our end of the year student-led conference where Kyle will be able to share with you his goals and the progress he has made.

cont.

I have attached a list of books by Eric Carle that you may want to pick up on your next trip to the library.

Sincerely,

Example 5-3: Checklist With Narrative

Yen has continued to work hard in the classroom and make progress. She attempts everything and asks many more questions if she doesn't understand what she is to do. She is interacting more with her peers and she now initiates more conversations. Yen is still quiet but is becoming more confident overall.

Yen writes much more freely and has improved at getting her thoughts on paper. She can write three or four sentences that are related uses consistent spacing, and capital and lower case letters appropriately. She has continued to increase the number of correctly spelled words in her writing also. She needs to concentrate on using the word board regularly to check her work and reread her work before sharing with an audience. Although reading remains a difficult area for Yen, she has shown some improvement. She continues to need practice and support. I am pleased to see that she continues to take home books on tape, and I encourage her to listen to them once a day for the entire week. She should also read her book bag books daily. She uses beginning and ending sounds including chunks of letters. Most recently, Yen is using rhyming words in patterns to help her predict new words. She should be talking about the stories and predicting what is going to happen in the story. What is most difficult for her is predicting words that might work in a sentence. Hopefully listening closely to the language in the books on tape will assist her and thus will help her to learn new and appropriate choices. She looks forward to reading with other students and finds it rewarding to share her materials in the "author chair." Individual reading conferences with me are a joy. She comes to each conference excited, eager, and ready to learn.

We are currently working on place-value activities in math. She is using concrete objects to do regrouping with addition and subtraction. She is making consistent and steady progress in this area. It appears that she is at ease with this subject and finds it rewarding. She is able to order numbers in proper sequence into the hundreds. She still confuses some names of numbers, but for the most part she finds math to be one of her strongest areas. Our new computer software which reinforces place value and many math concepts will be available to Yen. Money is another area that we have concentrated on this term, and Yen has been working hard to add coins in her head. This is something she should continue to practice at home using real coins. Her participation in the classroom store has helped out tremendously, but continual practice will only strengthen her skills and understanding. Yen is able to solve simple addition and subtraction story problems with ease. In the last few weeks, the children were given story problems that have extra or not enough information. They were asked to select only the appropriate information and identify the extra or to mention if there was not enough information to solve the problem. Yen is doing a fine job of selecting the appropriate information in simpler problems but still needs support with more complex problems. I hope this affords some understanding of her progress and offers a basis for our planning to meet her needs. I will look forward to talking with you about these matters.

Sincerely,

Language Arts Block	Needs Improvement	Some of the time	Most of the time	Consistently	
Reading					Individual reading conferences with me are a joy. She comes to each conference excited, eager, and ready to learn.
Applies Reading Strategies					
using pictures cues			X		Yen's reading continues to improve. She is able to:
uses phonetic cues				X	use beginning and ending sounds appropriately
uses context cues				X	use rhyming words and patterns to help her
self corrects/monitors		X			predict new words
Utilizes:					Yen continues to make progress in the areas of:
letter-sound recognition				X	monitoring and self correcting during reading
initial and final sounds				X	utiliizing pictorial information to aide in
reads with fluency	X				comprehension
reads with expression	X				
Comprehension					Additional improvement is needed in:
understands what is read	X				fluency/automaticity
can identify the main idea	X				expression
identifies supporting ideas	X				prediciting and retelling
Writing					
generates ideas		X			Yen's writing has improved. She is able to:
sequences events			X		* write 3 to 4 sentences related to a specific topic
uses semantic rules					* use spacing consistently
uses syntactic rules					* incorporate capitalization and punctuation
uses complete sentences			X		* use capital and lower case letters appropriately
applies spelling rules	X				
revise and edits work		X			Yen continues to make progress in the areas of:
Mechanic of writing					* ideation, revising and editing
uses capitialization				X	
uses punctuation				X	Additional improvement is needed in:
uses proper spacing				X	* applying spelling rules
Mathematics					
understands concepts of					Yen's mathematical ability continues to improve. She
addition				X	is making consistent and steady progress in the
subtraction				X	following areas:
multiplication					placing numbers in proper sequence
division					counting money
uses measurement forms					telling time
time			X		solve addition and subtraction problems
money				X	
weight and length					
uses					Her participation in the classroom store has helped out
problem solving strategies		X			tremendously. Continual practice in basic mathematical
reasoning			X		functions will strength her skills and understanding.
estimation					
sorting				X	

As we interviewed teachers about the types of reporting systems currently in existence in their buildings and districts, we learned that many were beginning to transition to more student-directed assessment practices. We were fortunate to have the opportunity to observe in several of these classrooms and to listen to their stories as they shifted toward narrative reporting. We offer the following responses, comments, suggestions. and recommendations that we gathered in our conversations with teachers.

Responding to Parental Concerns

With the emphasis on benchmarks and proficiency testing, parents are likely to want assurance that their child is progressing and meeting all expectations. Narrative reporting lends itself to open and ongoing communication with parents. The carefully crafted narrative will focus on what the child knows and what the child can do. The narrative can be written in a way that addresses parental concerns and questions in conjunction with other approaches such as conferencing or as a means of soliciting input. For example, the narrative can follow or precede a parent-teacher conference or the narrative can afford space for parents' concerns or comments on other matters.

Timetable

This is a decision that typically is made at the building or district level. A narrative can easily fit within any curriculum program. Most teachers cannot reasonably do a set of these kinds of narratives overnight. In our conversations with teachers, we found that most considered it less stressful when they alternated between the narrative report and the conference—either parent-teacher or student led. At one building, teachers completed narrative report cards twice a year, after the second and fourth grading terms. In place of the narrative reports during the first term, a parent-teacher conference was held in addition to a portfolio night and a curriculum night. In February, at the semester break, teachers facilitated student-led conferences at which goals were set and both completed and in-progress projects were shared.

Other teachers wrote narratives each grading term, but staggered the date each narrative would be completed and sent home. This enabled the teachers to complete a few narratives at a time rather than completing all reports by a particular date. A teacher following the format of sending a narrative home twice a year stated:

> We do it this way because we found that we were repeating ourselves in the conference. We had said everything in the narrative, and we really didn't have anything additional to say at the conference. So now we alternate the narrative with a conference. Both are time intensive, and it was redundant to write a narrative and meet with the parents in the same quarter.

We also found teachers who conducted student-led conferences in the fall, followed by a traditional checklist with a brief narrative the remaining three quarters.

Strengths of Narrative Reports

Narratives are most effective when they describe what is actually happening in the classroom. The narrative provides an opportunity to tell the parents the story of the day-to-day life in the classroom. Teachers can embed examples taken from everyday situations to emphasize a child's learning and growth. References made to the portfolio and projects that are inside the portfolio can be shared. Also, a grid of specific skills can be incorporated and explained in the narrative. A parent-teacher conference can be scheduled and specific questions and concerns can be addressed at this time if parents need more information. The narrative report is a great conversation starter. It helps the parents understand what activities motivate and engage their child.

Finding the Time to Write Narratives

Writing narratives can be ominous depending upon how they are approached. Teachers need to be realistic about what they can do. We recommend that in most classrooms, narratives be done at different times with students and perhaps only twice per year. We also recommend encouraging teachers to consider a shift from a narrative to either a dialogue journal or letter to the student or parent by e-mail or some other form. The narrative could be redeveloped as a letter to either the parent or child. It is important to focus an appropriate amount of time on each narrative. Many teachers find that by using a template they are able to organize information about each child quickly. Also, by using a template they are less likely to forget information. The template helps the teacher to focus on each area in a systematic fashion. Following is an example of such a template, developed for a class curriculum based on thematic units.

Example 5-4: Curriculum-Based Narrative Template

Student _____

Teacher _____

Dates covering _____

This semester I organized the class around _____. The students were involved in reading _____ selections that dealt with _____.

The focus of our discussion was _____. In conjunction with these units the students explored _____. As we explored these units, we attempted to relate their story problems in mathematics to _____.

Likewise, spelling followed from what was done in the unit. In conjunction with the spell-

---

cont.

ing, your child was encouraged to use these words in their reports. If you look through your child's portfolio, you will find examples of their explorations, including some of our afore-mentioned efforts.

As your child began the unit, s(he) specified an interest in the following _____, _____ as well as some goals_____ .

_____ (first name of child) was engaged in the planning, exploration, and development of various sets of materials. Among explorations were the following:

_____, _____, _____,

_____, _____, _____,

_____, _____, _____,

_____, _____, _____.

You may have seen many of them, but you might wish to review them again with your child in conjunction with the review of the portfolio. Be sure to listen to what your child was trying to do and what s(he) learned. In some cases s(he) achieved his/her goals; at other times goals changed. Also, remember that many of these pieces were under construction, so spelling and neatness may not have been stressed. Please contact me if you have any questions and to discuss ways we might work together to support his/her continued development.

_____ (first name of child) did a _____ job. In terms of traditional social studies skills, s(he) researched _____. His/her questions included _____.
In conjunction with these questions s(he) was able to develop an understanding of the _____. However, s(he) seemed to wrestle with _____.

In his/her reading s(he) _____ _____.

S(He) read and researched the following books and selections _____, _____, _____.

When I assessed how well s(he) was handling the material, s(he) read certain portions aloud and gave me a retelling. His/her retelling reflected _____. My checks on his/her oral reading indicated that s(he) was able _____ S(He) uses a variety of cuing systems (phonics, semantic or meaning, and syntax or grammar, including _____ .

His/Her writing reflected _____ plans beforehand and as s(he) writes _____.
Also, s(he) uses peer feedback for_____.

When s(he) revises s(he) _____.

In his/her mathematics, his/her reasoning reflected _____.

His/Her various creations (technology-based cities, reports, artwork) represented _____.

His/Her interactions with his classmates are _____.

His/Her portfolio represents _____. Please review the portfolio and let us know what you see as possible goals. Your child has reviewed his/her portfolio for himself/herself and has detailed his/her strengths and goals. (S)He tends to be self-critical, but when probed recognizes what s(he) has accomplished. His/Her goals tend to be emerging in ways that are concrete and add to his/her background and interests.

I am very pleased with the progress s(he) is making, especially in the following areas_____ _____,

I hope the report provides an overview of his/her progress and I look forward to talking with you about these matters. If you wish to contact me, please do so at _____.

The time given to teachers to complete the narratives differed by building and district. We learned that some teachers were given time each quarter to write assessments. With their students dismissed from school, the teachers had an opportunity to write letters to students and parents. Other teachers were given a professional day to complete the task. If these are not options, using recess, lunch breaks, and any other free moments has worked well. Narratives do take time to write and finding the time is a challenge.

Emphasis

Remember to describe each child by choosing different descriptors. This will keep each report unique. One of the strengths of the narrative is that it provides an individualized account of each student's progress. The template saves time but if overused, the narratives begin sounding alike. If the template is a rough outline of the areas to be covered, then the narratives remain unique. Having a list of descriptors available helps keep the language fresh. It is important to use language that is supportive and diplomatic. Information needs to be straightforward and honest, yet there can be legal ramifications if information is not clear or statements are made that cannot be backed up with evidence. So, read over each report for grammar errors as well as offensive language. Many teachers share ideas with peers and proofread each other's reports. Principals can also give an objective viewpoint. The child needs to be the focus of everything that one is thinking and doing. Finally, parents appreciate having a voice in their child's education. Asking parents for their input gives them an opportunity to share their thoughts and concerns.

Reactions to Narratives

As we observed several classrooms, we found it necessary to capture parent, teacher, and student comments about the narrative reports. We interviewed several individuals at random. Following is a synthesis of the types of comments we received.

Teachers

The teachers who either piloted or implemented narrative reports were overwhelmingly enthusiastic. They quickly responded that the narrative was well worth the time and effort, but they cautioned that a large drawback was that they were time intensive. Candice, a fifth-grade teacher shared, "I am able to communicate more thoroughly to each parent about their child. The parents have a much more comprehensive view of their child's growth and development. The narrative supports our school philosophy, which is to take each child where he is and move him forward."

Parents

Overall, we found that parents were enthusiastic about the narrative reports. They commented that the teachers seemed to know their child better when reporting progress in this way. A parent of a lower elementary student shared that "it [the narrative] was a very focused perspective on my child. I like the way the narrative emphasized change over time relative to herself rather than to everyone else in the class. I always read the teacher's comment section first when we had a checklist card with comments. This narrative is much more personal. My child takes the bus and I work full-time. I don't have much contact with the school or the teachers. This is a wonderful way to communicate with parents."

Students

Students seemed to like narratives as well. They liked reading about themselves and enjoyed the personal nature of the narrative. Sarah, a fourth-grade student, commented, "I also like grade cards. It sure feels great to get all pluses. My parents pay more attention to the report card than I do. I think it's more fun for them. I know what's going on and how I'm doing. It's my parents that want this information."

Reflections on Narratives

Narrative reports are one form of student-centered assessment that encourage ongoing dialogue among teachers, students, and parents. We found three types of narratives during our school visits: narratives written in story-like or letter format, narratives that describe thematic unit teaching, and a traditional report card with a narrative as a supplement. We learned that teachers and parents were interested in narrative reports since this form of assessment was more personal. They found that each narrative identified the individual child's interests and achievements in the work completed and learned in the classroom. This type of reporting, according to parents, was an excellent way to communicate with the teacher. The parents also liked the idea that their child's teacher really got to know their child. They found narrative reports positive and valuable to understanding their child's learning. Likewise, teachers were enthusiastic with this type of reporting. They related that narrative reports served as a vehicle to describe and explain a child's individual goals, interests, and achievements in a more individualized fashion. The narrative report documented a child's strengths and weaknesses in the work that was completed and learned in the classroom. The drawbacks to narrative reporting shared by teachers related to the amount of time to collect, document, and write the reports.

Six

The Report Dossier

History of the Report Dossier

The concept of the report dossier was developed several years ago while we were exploring the process of report card reform. At the time, we were visiting schools where assessment reform was in process, networking with teachers and researchers, and engaging in weekly dialogues. As we discussed reform issues, we also explored new possibilities. The report dossier emerged as one of the possibilities.

Several classroom teachers attended our weekly conversations. They were, in various ways, already utilizing more direct forms of assessment. Their students wrote in journals, collected their materials in portfolios or folders, and engaged in self-assessment and peer assessment. These teachers' input was crucial as we experimented with assessment possibilities. The emphasis of our discussion soon turned to what they thought about the roles of the various stakeholders in a student's assessment, what they would like to see happen in their own classrooms, and how we could help them achieve this.

Over the course of 2 years our conception of the dossier remained in flux as we received feedback from teachers, students, and parents. Even the name for what we were doing shifted: reflective binder, progress portfolio, assessment dossier, and, finally, report dossier. In fact, the elements of the dossier turned out to be much more important than the object itself. Each teacher incorporated those elements of the report dossier that worked in the culture of their classroom. In one class the students preferred to call their collection of assessment materials a binder; in another class the function of the portfolio already being used was simply shifted to incorporate the new materials and subsequently took on many of the elements of a report dossier. The teachers did not try to create identical assessment tools but instead constructed something new from within their learning community. Yet we found that we could all agree on several key theoretical concepts that guided our understanding and implementation of this new assessment tool.

Theoretical Construction of the Report Dossier

- Is grounded in and relevant to the lives of students
- Conveys a broad array of assessment information to the parents or guardians
- Enhances learning
- Serves as a good conversation starter
- Is woven into the day-to-day interactions
- Values the knowledge and experiences of teachers, students, and parents
- Engages in her reflection and in the setting and reaching of goals
- Involves all stakeholders in the process
- Creates a space for shared responsibility
- Increases the student's sense of agency
- Is recursive in nature
- Is emergent and constantly changing in response to feedback

Report dossiers were created to serve as prompts for conversations about assessment and goal setting. They are distinct from report cards, which tend to be concerned with either assessing the student's progress in a quantifiable manner or ranking the student's abilities in relation to peers. The report dossier is close in conception to a portfolio. It was evident as we visited schools that the term "portfolio" was being used to denote a wide range of assessment collections. In contrast to the traditional idea of the portfolio, we wanted to emphasize a particular function. The dossier is primarily about creating a space for a shared responsibility between parent, teacher, and student for assessment and learning. Using the materials collected, the student reflects on his or her learning and engages in assessment conversations with others. Teacher responses, peer responses, and parental responses all have a place in the dossier; and, therefore, it comes to represent a broad canvas of assessment focused on that particular student in the context of the learning community. The report dossier does not take the place of a portfolio, a journal, or a conference. In fact the report dossier works best when it interacts with these other elements.

The dossier tells the story of assessment, negotiated between all of the stakeholders; its narrative is multivoiced, offering all stakeholders a space in which to express their opinions. At the same time, central to the report dossier are the students themselves, who can create their sense of agency—their ability to make choices about what and how they learn—through taking the lead in writing the story of their learning in the dossier. Just as the portfolio creates a space for constituting new possibilities of self as learner (Clark, Chow-Hoy, Herter, Moss, & Young, 1996), the report dossier opens up new space for collaboration and dialogue about the student's learning.

The report dossier is also constructed within a particular classroom environment to fit the contexts of the site, so the exact materials included will reflect both the student and the classroom culture. The dossier must be developed around local needs, or it could easily become irrelevant. Therefore the report dossier reflects the teaching and learning occurring in the classroom. Some possible materials for inclusion in the dossiers are listed below.

What Goes in a Report Dossier?

- Overview of what will be studied
- Self-assessments: narratives and graphs
- Written goals
- Student work including drafts
- Revision sheets
- A dialogue journal
- Peer feedback
- Parent comment sheets
- Observations
- Anecdotal records

Issues of agency and goal setting are of central importance to our understanding of the role report dossiers play in a student's assessment. The overriding function of the dossier, however, is to engage the concerned parties in dialogue. Student and teacher, student and parent, parent and teacher, student and peers, student and self—in each instance the report dossier's value lies in its ability to start good conversations about assessment.

After working with the dossier for several months students in a fourth-grade classroom had become competent in discussing how they were assessing themselves. This competency developed in part because they were actively involved in the process, and in part because they were often engaged in dialogue relevant to learning and goal setting. In the conversa-

tion below, these students are immersed in a group discussion. The students are seated in a semicircle around the teacher, who has just asked what they think of the binders (report dossiers) they are now using. Both the binder and a checklist report card (which is issued district-wide) have recently been sent home to the parents. The teacher asked students what parents learned from each assessment tool:

Ryan: I think that the binder is better because you get to see more specific things, like instead of just having a plus or a minus, instead of four different scales, possible things, there are like infinite possibilities.

Teacher: 'Cause you have it in front of you?

Ryan: Yeah, and your parents can judge for themselves instead of having a preset judgment by you [the teacher].

Teacher: Good. Because the way I look at something might not be the same way you or your parents look at something and that's just part of life really 'cause everybody has different sets of values for what they believe. Anybody else have a comment on the binder? Scott?

Scott: You can kind of compare things and grade your own work. Like you can take your binder and your grade card and look at math and match it and see what you think, and how well you did.

These students have had a lot of experience with the subject matter. Although they have to continue using checklist-format report cards, for the culture of this particular community of learners the report card has been devalued and superseded by an assessment tool that is theoretically tied to a different understanding of learning.

Space for Assessment Conversations

The teachers who participated in this study were trying to connect assessment more clearly with the other things they were doing in the classroom. These classes already used an array of journals, language and writing folders, mathematics folders, portfolios, and conferences. The driving force behind the changes in their practices was the search for a way to lead the  students and the parents into constructive discussions about assessment.

In Tammy Harper's class, the report dossier was tied explicitly to conferencing. Tammy sends the dossier home several days before the parent-teacher conference, along with a letter from her, a conference sheet guide that includes teacher comments and a place for parent comments, and a self-assessment note written by the student.

November 3, 1995

Dear Parents,

Today your child is bringing home a binder which contains information about themselves this school year. It is a representation not only of academic work but work habits, social skills, and behavior. The binder is separated into five sections. Please take time to discuss each part with your child and have them share and tell you about the contents. You will also find my comments written on each child's self-evaluation. Please take into account the written comments and your child's body of work. There are also different gauges of growth, such as the graph in the analysis section.

The checklist for each student will be sent home Monday. Please remember the checklist is only one part of your child's progress. Keep in mind it is very difficult for me to summarize your child's work as a "+" or "-." Also, the checklist contains two additions. The first is points for returning homework. Each assignment is worth between 5 and 10 points. The points are given simply for returning homework. Points are not given for right or wrong answers, simply that it is attempted and brought back. The second addition is timed tests for multiplication facts. The facts are either mastered or are in progress. I cannot emphasize enough the importance of working on these facts at home if they are not mastered.

The value of the binder is dependent on your taking the time to have your child share with you. Please discuss with him/her and respond to the questionnaire included in the binder. This is an assignment for the students that will help them grow, too.

Finally, there will be a sign-up during conference time for parents to come in and share

---

cont.

with us. I know by the stories your children tell me and how wonderful they are that they must have talented parents. You could share a book, tell a story, teach us a dance, share a science experiment, share your career, share a hobby, play an instrument, or teach us a song! Whatever you would feel comfortable sharing. If you have some ideas but aren't sure, please ask!

I look forward to meeting with you at conferences.

Sincerely,

Tammy

In this class, parent response and interaction is regarded as integral to the learning process. Parents have always filled out a comment sheet on their child's learning in Tammy's class. This year they are asked to comment on the use of the binder as well. In addition to seeing the dossier at the conference, students in Tammy's class also took them home and went through the materials with their parents. When all of the binders were returned to school, Tammy held a group discussion. Most of the students were eager to share what their parents had done and said.

"She saw my graph and she said 'Oh, Sarah, that's you! That's definitely you!'"

"My mama agreed with me on it. She read it on her own and then she did it with me and then she had to fill out a little question sheet about how she felt how we were doing and other questions like that, and she went over it with my dad and my dad read it and then they read my self-evaluation and everything and said they agreed with me on that, and that's pretty much it."

One of the benefits of this process of having peers, teachers, and parents all read the materials is that the students come to recognize something about the different audiences they are writing for. At times this can backfire. Knowing that they are writing the dialogue journal for the teacher, who will respond accordingly, students might try to simply write what they think the teacher wants to hear. Still, a student who engages in "meaningless" writing (writing to please or only to complete an assignment) is likely to engage in other behaviors that indicate a lack of motivation to learn for the sake of learning. If this is the case, the teacher can talk with the student to find out what kind of learning would be more interesting or to see if there is some other problem eclipsing the student's desire to learn.

In Barbara's fifth-grade class student-teacher assessment conversations were ongoing. These conversations often started out with the teacher asking questions designed to lead from behind: "But how will I know if your writing has improved?" "What do you see that you are doing better?" "What can I do as a teacher to help?" However, the student is situated as the expert on her own work and its assessment. In Tammy's class, in addition to discussions, the students and the teacher keep dialogue journals. The students write about what they have been reading and what they are thinking. The teacher then responds in the journal. When the dialogue journal succeeds, and it often does in Tammy's class, a number of threads of discussion will intertwine in the journal with the teacher and student engaging in thoughtful and recursive explorations.

In the report dossier, students collect multiple revisions of their writings, helping students learn about the process of editing and revising. In Tammy's class students often include in the binder a piece of writing, a revision sheet, and a revision. The revision sheet contains questions that reinforce several concepts: that writing is a process that necessitates revision, that things are often written for an audience and feedback from that audience might improve the writing, and that writing is never really finished because each reading has the potential to change its meaning.

- What revisions have you made on your piece?
- Who suggested the revision?
- What do you like about this piece?
- What other changes might you make?
- Who have you read your work to?
- What were their reactions?

Because it is a process, drafts and revisions are important. Multiple drafts suggest process over product. Multiple drafts and revisions allow learners to examine the strategies they have employed and the decisions they have made—what they have learned, what they are in process of learning, and what they are ready to learn.

Students do not just evaluate where they are currently. They examine what they have learned, how they have learned, and what they might have done differently. By gaining additional insights from their audiences, they are constantly confronting new possibilities. They experiment, revise, and, most of all, learn new strategies that can then be applied to other situations. Learning in these classrooms might best be described as ongoing collaboration or negotiation. Ideally, insight is gained into the students' learning strategies and knowledge, which in turn should guide the curriculum.

Agency and Shared Responsibility

The report dossier is in many ways similar to a portfolio. The student knows best what materials are important to his or her self-identity as a learner, which is what a portfolio is all about. With a portfolio, the student is the owner and creator of the body of work he or she wishes to use to highlight his or her own learning. Regrettably, many schools utilize teacher selection of materials, thereby negating one of the primary benefits of portfolio systems. The report dossier takes on a different function: that of seeking to enhance participation in assessment conversations. Students, parents, and teachers all have the opportunity to engage in the analysis and decision-making, allowing multiple voices and sides of the story to interact. Assessment becomes a shared responsibility, a collaboration. Ultimately, though, the dossier is under the student's control.

> Problem: How do you Represent Collaborative Projects in the Report Dossier?
>
> We do a lot of cooperative learning projects—they take photos of the project and the student writes about what's going on. That way they have a record of what they did in the group even if they don't have the final project, and it's especially helpful for the parents to see what they are doing in groups 'cause a lot of the parents aren't able to visit here at school. (Barbara)

The report dossier is designed to allow new possibilities for students to don the mantle of expert and become proprietors of their own assessment. Many of the items that the students put in their dossier are self-generated, often after a group dialogue or a conversation between teacher and student. In practice some of the materials are preestablished but most are open-ended forms filled out by the student: peer review sheets, revision sheets, and self-assessments such as "What I Do Well in Writing."

Significantly, students who have been actively involved with constructing their dossiers can lead you through the materials, tell you how they have improved, where they want to be by the end of the year, and how they are going to get there. The teacher in the new discourse becomes both a facilitator and a collaborator, helping the student organize, providing feedback, and engaging in dialogue. Parents are still the primary audience for the information found in the dossier, but they also become collaborators in the learning and assessing process.

When we were looking for volunteers to lead us through their dossiers, one of the first to raise her hand was a young woman the teacher had described as very shy. In fact the teacher was surprised that she volunteered. But the students by this point knew what was in their dossiers and why things were included, and for this student such knowledge boosted her confidence. She took us through her dossier step by step. She explained what each item meant, how she was doing, the goals she had set for herself, why she had chosen certain works to include in her binder over others, and how she had revised her writings after receiving feedback from the teacher and her peers.

Assessment and Goal Setting

Everyone in Tammy's class has a large blue binder that they have decorated and personalized with stickers, drawings, and names. These binders are kept in a bookshelf near the art and writing supplies. Though it does not happen everyday, students will occasionally go to their dossier to add something they have been working on. Sometimes this is student initiated, other times the teacher suggests that they might want to include something in their binder. Occasionally, the entire class will work on similar projects to put in their binders.

Some of the materials in the dossiers are forms generated by the teacher or by the students. These forms tend to be open ended and contextualized to fit the culture of the class. Tammy has found that prefabricated forms from other sources might lead students in directions that have nothing to do with the learning that takes place in her classroom. One form the students do put in their binder is filled out at the end of each nine-week period. The form asks the students what they learned, what they do well, what they need help with, and what they are most proud of.

Barbara uses a similar sheet in her classroom with the questions, "What did I do well? What did I learn? What other things would I like to learn?" Each Monday, Barbara sends home a folder. From this folder the students choose the materials to put in their dossier or portfolio. When she first started using the form, Barbara tried to have the students complete one for every item that went into their portfolio.

> Last year I had my students fill out this form on everything in their portfolio, why they included it, why they were proud of it, how they were going to improve it . . . and they had to do that on every piece, and what I found was that the students just filled in the blanks and didn't really think about it. So now I only have them fill out this form on a couple of the pieces and when we have our conference those are the pieces we talk about.

Many teachers have expressed concern that when engaging in discussions of their own assessment, students will give the teacher the answers they think he or she wants, will not take the exercise seriously, or will find stock phases to repeat over and over. Such fears are not totally unfounded. Teachers faced with filling out forms on every student in the class at the end of a grading period may also fall into the trap of repeating standard, almost meaningless phrases over and over.

One way Tammy has attempted to handle this situation is to have these forms in a folder hanging on the wall next to the binders. When a student wants to comment on his or her own work or suggest a revision to a peer, these forms are available. The form for peer feedback has proven to be especially popular. Students assert that using the revision sheet has actually improved their writing and editing skills.

Assessment that is tied to learning is necessarily a reflective practice. Students can take more risks in their learning and experimentation when these are viewed not as products to be judged but as opportunities in learning. Another activity that these teachers integrate into the binders is the setting of goals. Goal setting might benefit students by enhancing their self-reflexivity. For the teacher engaging in goal setting with students the activity might give insights into the students' world. On the other hand, formalizing the goal-setting process might lead to students saying what they think the teacher wants them to say, or result in redundant and repetitive goals. Perhaps the best way to prevent this is to dialogue about the process.

Students in Tammy's class set goals detailing what they want to accomplish every 9 weeks. However, because learning is constant and is being informed by all the conversations the student is having about assessment, they are constantly engaged in more informal goal setting. Questions to consider are:

- What is the purpose of goal setting?
- Who sets these goals?
- How did students get where they are?
- How can they reach where they want to be?
- What are the benefits of goal setting for students? For teachers?

- Should goal setting be integral to assessment conversations?
- How often should students engage in goal setting?
- Should they concentrate on short-term goals, long-term goals, or a combination?

Students in Tammy's class also write several narrative self-evaluations. One important function of these assessments is that they allow the student to reflect on their own learning. Over time, as students become accustomed to assessment dialogues, these self-assessments can become increasingly informative. In one narrative included in the dossiers, students wrote about their attitudes and work habits in relation to reading, writing, and mathematics.

> I like to write nature and animal poems, but I think I need to work on other genres.

> I like to do a lot of reading but I still think that I could work on exploring the meaning of the words.

> I have a tendency to get off task, I used to think that you could only be friends by showing off, but I am working on it.

> I can get very disorganized and interrupting. My attitude is pretty good, I think, but last year I didn't seem to do well on my homework, but I've returned my homework every day almost and I'm proud of it.

Narratives help the student organize their own understanding of how they are learning and can convey this information to the parents as well as the teacher. These assessments can address the potential and the identity of the learner in ways a grade never could.

Self-Graphing

One day during a class discussion Tammy brought up the idea of self-graphing. The students had been doing some graphs in mathematics and science so they were familiar with the idea of graphing. They had also been engaged in a variety of self-assessments. Now they discussed how they might combine the two elements. Several academic subjects were

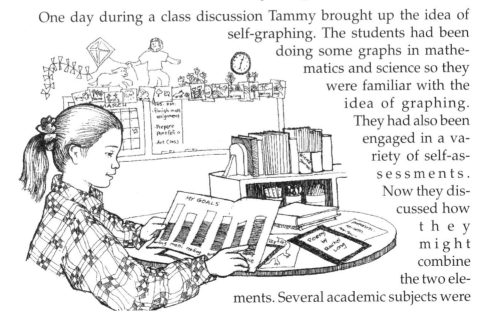

suggested at the outset and these were agreed upon, but students also felt that it was important that they include elements of the whole person. They wanted to assess themselves as learners in all aspects of their lives. When they had added all the subjects they wanted to include as a group, they determined that the last slot should be left blank for individuals to add something important to them personally. The students also discuss-ed how they might use different colors to represent different aspects of their abilities and growth. The students thought that it would be infor-mative to distinguish schoolwork from the "everyday" and from plea-sure. They also wanted to include another color to distinguish where they wanted to be at the end of the nine-week session. They decided that each student would design a graph to suit his or her own needs.

After completing the graphing process (Figure 6-1), Sarah explained that she had chosen blue for every day, green for pleasure, brown for schoolwork, and purple for where she would like to be at the end of the 9 weeks. Then while she was making the graph she decided to add another color. She asserted,

> I have lots of friends and I think there's a lot of warmth in there (yellow is warmth) I see my friends everyday (there is blue filling part of the column for friendship and yellow in the other part), but I think I could work on being nice to my friends a lot more (an extra inch of purple is added at the top of the column).

Sarah holds up her graph and points to the column labeled "family":

> Most of it is yellow for warmth, and some of it is green for pleasure. I think that I am really in touch with my feelings, but I put that I could improve some because you always need to work on that.

This is the point at which the teacher or parent can discuss with Sarah what she might do to improve. What does she think could be worked on? The last column is perhaps the most interesting because this is where the students can choose something that does not relate to school at all.

Students also wrote narrative goals that they kept in their dossiers. These goals were meant to be viewed as dialogue starters—students think about where they are and where they want to be when they are writing and designing their graphs, but they still need to discuss how they are going to get there and how they got to where they are.

These students already have a good understanding of their own learn-ing and assessments when they reach the teacher-student conference. Both Tammy and Barbara view the conversations that occur at these confer-ences as essential to assessment, helping the students learn more about how to put into words what they are doing, and helping the teacher learn where the student is and what help they might need. Barbara said, "If I just looked at what they wrote I don't think I would learn as much. You need a conversation."

Figure 6-1. Sarah's Graph

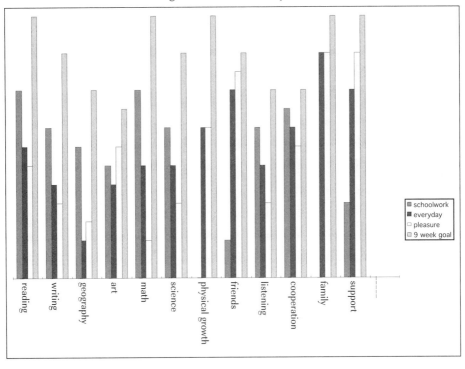

Feedback From Parents

The parents were, in general, quite pleased with the dossiers. Most parents appreciated the opportunity to go over schoolwork with their child. They were used to seeing the schoolwork come home, and some had even made efforts to look at any materials that came through the door. But this was different; these materials were chosen by the student in negotiation with their teacher to best represent and assess what they had learned over the course of the year. The students had actually reflected on how this work related to their overall learning, and based on this information had set goals for future learning.

When the dossiers were sent home with the students, a parent comment sheet was sent with it. Questions on the parent comment sheet included:

- What positive growth have you observed in your child?
- What are you most impressed with in his/her work?
- What would you like to see him/her improve?
- How does the information in the binder compare to the checklist you usually receive?
- What else would help you understand your child's growth and what he/she needs to improve?

Parents emphasized a number of benefits:

> The data in the binder express a deeper and broader profile of David's skills, abilities and triumphs.

> It gives me a better idea of the caliber of work that he is producing or capable of producing.

> I think that by involving the students in goal setting you help them grow intellectually. Congratulations for your initiative!

> It is helpful to see Katie's work, also to see her assessments of where she is, what she likes, and where she feels she needs to be.

> This binder provides a much more complete picture of what Adam is doing in school and how he is growing.

> The dossier makes it easier to discuss his work with him in that references can be drawn upon.

> It is nice to go over it at home a couple of days before the conference, usually I don't see samples of her work until the day of the conference.

> The best aspect for me is Sebastian's analyses of himself, his work, and what needs to improve.

> You give us exactly what we need. Talking with him and talking with you helps us put the pieces together.

> We were very impressed by his self-analysis (in the binder) and by your summation as well.

> It was valuable to see the work in context with the assignment and with Allie's goals.

> It is specific and hands-on—I like having the opportunity to sit with Sarah and discussing—reflecting prior to the conference. It seems like I know what has been going on so when we meet we can talk in more specifics.

> Good to see an evaluation based on actual examples.

Nevertheless, there were parents who were not satisfied with the changes in assessment. At least one parent wanted to know where her daughter stood in relation to the peer group, and wished that there would be a standard curriculum and mastery of certain skills at certain specified times. Surprisingly, many suggestions involved expanding the dossier to include more elements such as video and visuals. Several also commented that the dossier had emphasized writing and reading and should include more mathematics, sci-

- broader profile
- better idea of abilities
- meaningful in its specificity
- student involvement
- goal setting
- enhancement of discussion with student
- contextualization of the work
- hands-on practicality

ence, and art. One parent suggested including more information relative to change over time. Another thought that it would be useful to send the dossier home more than once during the 9-week session.

Reflections on the Report Dossier

Students create report dossiers in collaboration with their teachers and peers allowing space for parental response. Dossiers contain many possible artifacts from multiple drafts of writing to pictures of collaborative projects. It also contains reflections on the student's work from the teacher, peers, parents, and the student himself or herself.

Life in the constantly changing, technology-centered 21st century requires that children become flexible enough to learn and to adapt to new technology as it becomes available. When students become highly motivated, self-directed learners, they are developing lifelong skills that will help them to be successful. The report dossier supports the development of self-direction in learning through giving students the opportunity to consider their growth in relation to feedback from those who care most about them—their teachers and their parents.

Seven

Digital Assessments

Introduction

In a third-grade class in San Diego County, California, the students select work throughout the year to include in their portfolios. Using a template created by the teacher, the students take samples from their working portfolio and scan them into an electronic showcase portfolio. They then engage in self-evaluation and make connections between the samples from different content areas.

In a middle-school classroom in central Ohio, the students have created websites as a class project. These websites are presented to the other students, who evaluate and provide peer feedback. The presentations are videotaped and later exhibited to parents during an open house.

High school students in Alaska have designed exhibition portfolios that they place on the school website. Local professionals and admissions officers from colleges and universities visit the website and then communicate with students via e-mail about their work and possibilities for the students' future.

These are just a few of the many examples of the ways new forms of technology are affecting teaching, learning, and assessment. The potential for the digital world to influence assessment in positive ways depends on much more than wiring schools and purchasing hardware. There is enormous potential for these electronic assessments to extend dialogue and partnerships between students, teachers, caregivers, and other stakeholders.

Technology and Assessment

Technological changes are constantly influencing shifts in the ways we learn and assess, the means by which we communicate, and the lenses through which we view our own and other people's work. In terms of assessment, the focus of computer technology has often been on efficiency rather than on qualitative possibilities. However, some software developers have realized that there is much potential in electronic assessment options. Even more significantly some teachers have explored ways of using technology to support alternative forms of assessment in their classrooms.

Whatever types of assessing are being used in the classroom, there is likely software that is designed to aid the teacher and the student, as well as technologies not specifically designed for assessment purposes that nonetheless have enormous potential to affect the ways we teach and learn. There is currently much experimentation with digital portfolios and the use of technology to enhance student exhibits and presentations of learning.

Ideally, a classroom that has integrated technology into its day-to-day activities and assessments would have at least one computer for every four students, a scanner, web access, and a number of authoring software packages such as Hyperstudio, Microsoft Word, Frontpage, Netscape Composer, KidPix. A variety of assessment templates would be helpful, especially those created by teachers in the classroom and those that are customizable and adaptable to context.

Ways Technology Has Impacted Assessment

- Electronic support of existing assessments

- Tools for efficiency of analysis and summarizing

- Facilitated access and interchange

- Expanded repertoire of ways of knowing and assessing

- Shifts in conceptions about learning and assessing

Many of the software programs specifically designed for assessment purposes are meant to increase efficiency of analysis and summary. Electronic grade cards, for example, can sort and average grades efficiently. They are also potentially adaptable and customizable to fit the local context. Some of these programs allow teachers to add comments that might be linked directly to the individual's grade or even directly to a scanned image of a product.

As for portfolio assessment, massive amounts of student work can be stored on a single CD-ROM or disk, relieving many storage and accessibility problems. Students can also keep the original work while the school keeps a virtual copy. The student could take a digital portfolio with him or her for all 12 grades, revisiting and making connections between work accomplished over the years. The use of technology could provide virtually instantaneous comparisons of a student's work over time and through multiple revisions.

Technology also has the potential to facilitate greater access and interchange among members of the learning community. The possibility for input and communication is tremendous. A number of programs allow the audience to participate in the assessment by commenting on what they are viewing; and when parents, students, peers, and other audiences have these materials at their fingertips, they are more likely to interact and dialogue. With the student's portfolios from each year on a single disk or intranet, the student and teacher can readily access the information needed to look at a student's performance longitudinally. The teacher is also better able to engage in assessment dialogues with the student if the materials are readily at hand and if there is a locally generated template for response. Some electronic grade cards are also accessible to caregivers with a modem and a password. However, with this level of accessibility, issues of privacy also become prominent. If the portfolio is

openly available on the internet, serious decisions have to be made as to what information should be included.

Expanding Repertoires of Ways of Knowing and Assessing

How do we make sure that students are partners in assessment? How do we get students to look at themselves over time to make connections in self-assessment? Helping students organize their materials digitally can be done using a variety of platforms, but some are more likely to help students look at themselves through different lenses.

Technology allows links to be made between a variety of media including audio, video, and graphics. Teachers using letter grades can include comments on the grading, extenuating circumstances, and evidence to support the grade. Electronic portfolios can combine all types of multimedia work and make interconnections between these elements. Technology allows for the inclusion of more performance-based materials in the student portfolio. One of the largest bonuses of technology is that it allows multiple links between assessment materials. Not only can student work be included but also various drafts and revisions, comments from others (such as teachers, peers, parents, or outside audiences), rubrics, self-assessments, goals, or learning objectives. All of these assessment materials can be tied together in multiple ways in the ongoing process of assessment. The links between the various elements become more explicit when they are interconnected with the click of a button. Hypermedia therefore encourages the students to make connections between various elements of their learning and their assessment as a complex system.

Digital Portfolios

Characteristics of Digital Portfolios
- Integrate multiple media: photos, audio, video, graphics
- Provide multiple paths through the work using links as an effective form of cross-referencing (collaborative projects and interdisciplinary samples)
- Provide support for reflection
- Enable sharing of responses
- Provide access to multiple perspectives
- Stimulate dialogue
- Promote student ownership
- Enable multiple copies for student, teacher, and job or college applications
- Build on background knowledge
- Encourage revision and self-assessment
- Encourage the exploration of possibilities
- Help manage the massive storage problem
- Provide an instant comparison of work from all 12 years
- Provide easy means of keeping track of student information
- Provide simple and fast interface to find information
- Are interactive
- Emphasize assessment as a process

The terms *electronic portfolio, digital portfolio,* and *computer-based portfolio* tend to be used interchangeably. The use of computer technology to enhance portfolio assessment has a number of benefits. Locating, storing, and sorting information becomes simple. Student samples, teacher comments, anecdotal records, emergency information, rubrics, grades, or whatever information and assessments the school system, teacher, or student deems important can be included and easily accessed. While space has proven to be a problem in many classrooms, especially in cases where the portfolio follows the student from kindergarten through 12th grade, with the electronic portfolio this becomes less of a problem.

For schools that have the hardware, the storage of digitized assessment information is more economical and efficient. This also means that an eighth-grade language arts teacher who would like to trace a student's writing history will have these materials on hand. Many teachers have been reluctant to let the portfolios travel home with the student because they are irreplaceable if lost. When digital portfolios are used, there can be a school copy and another copy the student can take with him or her to work on at home, to show to parents, and so on. With contemporary technology, transferring a portfolio onto a CD-ROM costs only a few dollars. This means that digital portfolios can be reproduced not only for the school and the student but also for job or college applications. A student who has a vested interest in showing his or her best work for a particular audience is likely to put more effort into self-assessment.

The digital portfolio can also be used to incorporate multiple media in a single document, media that can be linked in a variety of ways that make sense to the student. Alternate formats including video, audio, and collaborative projects can now be included and easily viewed in conjunction with reflections, grades, and comments by parents, teachers, or peers. Links can be made between objectives and assignments, drafts and revisions. In schools moving toward standards-based or outcomes-based assessment, multiple links can be made between individual outcomes and student products. In this way, the work and the evaluation are placed in context and can be viewed as a process. Here are some examples of home pages and links.

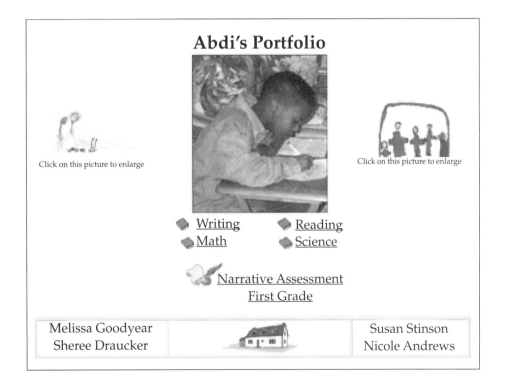

Welcome page for student digital portfolio: Kindergarten

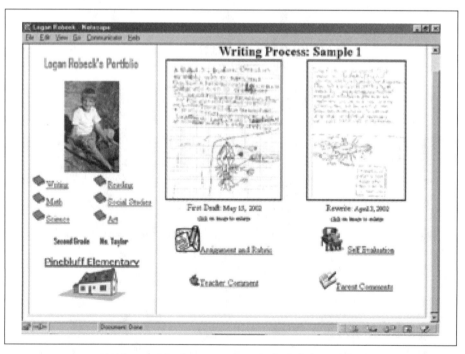

Writing samples in a second grader's digital portfolio

The Coalition of Essential Schools' Digital Portfolio, which has been piloted in schools in Kentucky, New Hampshire, and New York, identifies the student and the school on the opening page. The portfolio includes school learning goals and outcomes for each content area, as well as benchmark performances—such as samples from previous students. The core content of the portfolios is student demonstrations of their work and can include presentations, research projects, or tests.

Each goal has a table of contents with links that take the viewer to demonstrations of student performance. These might include text, graphics, video, or audio component. Some performances might be linked to more than one goal, something that print portfolios would have trouble achieving. The actual assessment and comments can also be linked to each performance providing more context. On each performance page there is an evaluation button which takes the viewer to a list of evaluators; clicking on one of these, in turn, will take the viewer to the evaluator's comments, rubrics, and grades.

The teacher who creates templates specifically suited to a classroom has the greatest chance of meeting the needs of the students in that class. For example, students in East Syracuse-Minoa High School in New York have worked with a template they created on Hyperstudio, which they call "The Portfolio Manager." The students are in charge of creating and maintaining portfolios that are begun in the sophomore year. These portfolios are designed to be sent to college admissions offices and potential employers.

Using Electronic Portfolios in a Third-Grade, Bilingual Classroom

This example from San Diego County, California, takes a closer look at how a teacher designed digital portfolio templates to meet the needs of his students. Eric, a third-grade teacher in a year-round school with a Latino population of 92 percent, is developing electronic portfolios with his students. Eric became interested in portfolios as a way to better capture his students' capabilities on an ongoing basis. He is also very interested in exploring the possibilities of technology for promoting the literacy development of young learners. Developing electronic portfolios seemed like a way to merge the two interests.

Eric has assisted students with collecting their work samples since January 1997. He explains to us that he helped them create two types of portfolios, a working and a showcase portfolio. He then helped the students convert the showcase portfolio to a digital format.

After categorizing work samples with his students (including content categories like mathematics, writing, social studies, and extracurricular items), Eric helps his students select samples from their working portfolio to include in their showcase portfolio. He found that before long students begin to realize the power of personalizing their portfolios, and he believes this helps them to invest in the process. Next, he created a self-evaluation form that asked students four identical questions for each category in their portfolio (Figure 7-1).

**Figure 7-1. Student Self-Evaluation/Conference Form—Mathematics
(Spanish as used in my class)**

Nombre _____ Grado_____ Fecha_____

Mi Portafolio: Sección Matemáticas

1. ¿Cuál es el título o descripción de tu trabajo de Matemáticas?
   _____
   _____

2. ¿Por qué escogiste este trabajo para tu portafolio electronico?
   _____
   _____
   _____
   _____

3. ¿Qué hiciste bien en este trabajo y/o qué te enseña de tí?
   _____
   _____
   _____

4. ¿ Qué podrías a hacer major la próxima vez o en el futuro?
   _____
   _____
   _____
   _____

A student chooses samples of her work in mathematics, writing, and social studies, and then she responds to the same questions about each section. Eric feels that this facilitates higher-order thinking and encourages self-reflection by his students. At this point, the student portfolios are ready to be converted into a digital format. Eric explains the process in this way:

> The next step was converting the work samples and other items into digital format. This has proven to be the most time-consuming part of the process. One of the most important realizations I made was that I needed a template that I could use for all the students. Early on, I had intentions of being very democratic and allowing every student to choose

his or her own graphics, colors, designs, etc. I soon realized that third graders can't choose those sorts of things very quickly and instead want to try every color and look at every graphic, and I've got thousands of them! I ended up adapting a sample on the Hyperstudio CD that is called "Our Class Album: An Electronic Portfolio" which uses the same title page or home page for every student, but with their own picture and name on it.

Eric realized that the number of choices grading and assessment technology offers classroom teachers was part of both its power and complexity. He concludes his explanation of the process in this way:

> I initially created this template with two students, a boy and a girl, then used those templates with the "save as" feature of the computer to make initial portfolios for the other students. Doing this saved a lot of time and gave each student a base to start from.

Eric's home pages served as one of the templates for the rest of the class (see figure 7.2).

Figure 7.2. Eric's Home Page

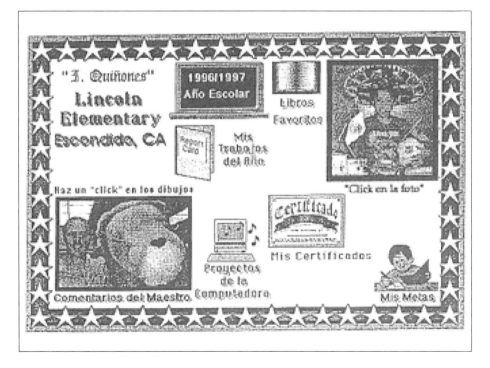

His next task was to convert the samples from his students into an electronic format. He explained this to me:

> To digitize the work samples, I used a combination of scanner for writing or art projects that were small enough to be scanned, the digital

camera for student pictures and pictures of larger art or social studies projects, the video camera for student videos . . . I did most of the camera work myself but also trained several students who showed an interest in technology how to use the scanner and put samples in the portfolio.

From this account, two salient points emerge that indicate the potential power and value of electronic portfolios. First, these portfolios become a space in which students have an experience of transmediating one form of their work into another (e.g., an art project such as a model or drawing into an electronic representation). Second, the use of technology encourages learners to develop their own expertise and assist their peers in the assessment process as well. Getting students involved in the assessment process is a cornerstone of learner-directed assessment. As we seek to move our students towards working with multiple ways of representing knowledge and achievement, assessment practices that move from physical samples to electronic media provide opportunities for reflecting on their work and the work of their peers in new ways. For example, Eric includes video text of students in their portfolios and then adds video of himself commenting on their portfolios. Students are able to access these videos for themselves and their parents, and continue a conversation about their own achievement. This layering of assessment texts and comments is more than just a technological trick; it encourages learners to continue to reflect both on their work and their assessments of their work, and it creates new spaces for self-expression and critique.

Instructional Effects in Eric's Classroom

Eric saw changes in his class in three arenas: instruction, assessment, and classroom environment. He believes his use of electronic portfolios helped him shift from what he refers to as "sage of the stage" to "a more student-centered, constructivist type of instruction" that allowed students to direct their own learning. He describes some of these changes:

> The portfolio is a more personal type of project that requires its creator to evaluate and make decisions about its contents. I found that I did a lot more initial modeling of skills like categorizing, evaluating, and helping with selection of the work samples, conferencing, and assisting in using technological tools. After I modeled, the students worked independently, with me acting as facilitator and coach.

In terms of classroom assessment, Eric explained that he was "able to more easily observe students working on their portfolios and using computers." He noted diverse strategies for selection and categorization (some methodically used self-stick notes while others worked haphazardly) and connected these with differences among learning styles. He also related how listening to their justifications for selecting work in a conference setting instructed him on what his students valued and their processes of metacognition.

Finally, he saw himself giving up control while his students gained control over their own learning. Although this was not easy, for a teacher who was used to directing the flow of talk and interaction, in the end he said

> One of the most valuable things about using this type of portfolio assessment is that it empowers students and teaches them to be independent workers and thinkers, but also to work and cooperate with other students.

Overall, Eric found using electronic portfolios to be valuable for his students and himself as a teacher. Both shared in the learning that was constructed from the rich teacher-student interactions that emerged from implementing electronic portfolios. These students' voices emerged as they began to understand their own growth and achievement. Eric began to rethink his role as a facilitator or coach while gaining new insights into the complexities of student learning and assessment.

Lasercard Portfolios

Marshall High School in Portland, Oregon, is utilizing a system of student assessment in which each student has an ID-size digital card use at computer stations throughout the school to examine and make changes to the electronic portfolios. Some of the information is actually encoded on the card, which can hold three megabytes of material. Other resources and more sensitive materials are stored on a computer, with the lasercard linking the user to relevant sources.

Each card is imprinted with a picture of the student, his or her signature, name, and student ID number. Among other things, the lasercards contain the electronic portfolio, schooling history (transcript information, attendance, and entry and withdrawal information), health records, extracurricular activities in which the student participated, and any community services performed by the student. Only best samples of student work as determined by the student and teachers are included in the portfolios. Photographs of student projects, scanned artwork, and word processing documents are just a few examples of the types of work that can be stored in the portfolio section of the lasercard. Information can be put on the card in several different ways: with digital cameras, scanners, or downloaded from a computer.

With this system students are able to organize, store, and quickly access all of their best work. In order to access the information on the card, a special card reader is necessary. In some cases, sensitive information is not actually stored on the card. Instead, a pointer on the card indicates where the information is stored on the intranet. Besides keeping data on students, the laser card gives students and staff access to a resource database that includes lesson plans, bibliographies, and other curricular support materials.

Cards are updated from the central repository, a designated computer at Marshall High School. The student inserts the card into the special optical read/write drive, enters a password, and automatically updates the card with the most current information. To access the information, the card can be taken to a lasercard reader station.

By the time a student graduates, he or she will have a ready product to show colleges and potential employers. Copies of the portfolio are sent on disk, as a hard copy, faxed, or transmitted via modem upon request as long as the student (and parent/guardian if the student is under 18 years) gives permission. Faculty have their own lasercards that provide access to all their students' files on the computer.

Prepackaged Templates

Although classroom teachers like Eric who have some experience with technology can create assessment templates suited to their particular students, there are also companies and researchers who prepare ready-made portfolio templates. Some of these electronic portfolios are rather rigid in their construction; and although they allow the teacher to plug in a variety of data and work samples, there is less possibility of gearing the process toward particular classroom needs. Other templates are quite flexible and the companies that design them will often cater to the specific needs of a school system.

Aurbach's Grady Profile is a digital portfolio system made in a hypercard format. The Grady Profile is meant to encourage student self-assessment, parent-teacher conferencing, and the use of multimedia to capture and store diverse student work. In addition it provides an environment conducive to organizing and evaluating work samples. Using HyperCard stacks, the program facilitates tracking and collecting performance over time. Teachers and students are encouraged to observe, take notes, record audio and video, and insert data in order to present multiple facets of student performance. Rubrics and checklists are also encouraged. The Aurbach website details additional information: http:// www.aurbach.com/form_gpdemo.html.

Scholastic's Electronic Portfolio emphasizes that the portfolio will create a cumulative record of student growth from pre-kindergarten through grade 12. The portfolio can manage images, photographs, sample work, and video in addition to all the information that is standard in a cumulative record. Scholastic stresses:

> This capacity enables the teacher to capture and monitor both process and best pieces within the same portfolio. The electronic portfolio has provided teachers, students, and parents with access to rapid comparisons of students' progress and comprehensive capacities for reporting and monitoring student performance.

Scholastic has also built in the capacity for easy transfer from computer to video so that the teacher can send a videotape home to the parents with selections or even the entire portfolio to facilitate interaction.

Sunburst's Learner Profile stresses teacher use of hand-held Apple Newtons to observe and collect data in the classroom. The information is then transferred to a hard drive where the electronic management system collects and reports data. The company stresses the compatibility of Learner Profiles with IEPs (Individual Education Plan), and that the program not only allows for documenting the process of learning but also that it can quantify many qualitative aspects of learning. The Sunburst website is: http://www.sunburst.com/schoolhouse/learnerprofile/

Criteria for Evaluating Electronic Portfolios

- What kind of information is available about the student?
- Does the electronic portfolio support multimedia (video, audio, graphics, etc.)?
- How easy is it to navigate through the student's work?
- Are responses to and reflections on student work supported by the software? Whose responses (teacher, parent, peers, self, etc.)?
- What sort of student work appears in the portfolio?
- What other types of assessment are integrated into the portfolio (rubrics, checklists, teacher comments, self-assessments, etc.)?
- Who controls this portfolio? Who has ownership of the materials? (Teacher, administrators, parent, student, etc.)
- Does the portfolio contain best samples only or various drafts and revisions of a project?

Presentations

In addition to enhancing traditional and more direct assessments, computer technology can provide digital environments conducive to presenting and exhibiting student materials in a variety of ways: to a graduation committee, at a parent-student conference, to peers, or to outside audiences via the web.

At Kilbourne Middle School in Worthington, Ohio, grade 7 students in a language arts class created websites that they presented to other students in the class who evaluated their work. These presentations were videotaped and subsequently shown to parents at an open house. The presentation took on additional depth as a result of these multiple layers. Students received feedback from parents and the teacher on both their presentations and their evaluations of their classmates. The fact that parents were able to view not only the product but also the process of peer review added an exciting dimension. Technology here is being used in ways that promote dialogue and provide incentive for student effort.

At Kroc Middle School in San Diego County, the educational technologist has created a Hyperstudio template for transforming the traditional district portfolio into a digital portfolio. This allows multimedia aspects to be included. On their website the school asserts that:

> A typical Kroc portfolio might contain an original poem with recorded voice from English, a database of famous world leaders from History, a spreadsheet of a personal budget from math, an animation of a science project, a digitized image (Quicktake) of a race from P.E. and a scanned image of a test from Spanish.

Materials are stored on a zip drive and then placed on the computer laboratory server. Students add reflections on their work directly to the electronic portfolio. The portfolios can be saved to disk and distributed with a free run-only version of Hyperstudio. Alternatively, they can be put on the internet.

Students also present their portfolios in front of students, teachers, parents, and community representatives. Presentations take place in a hall with the portfolio displayed on a large screen. Students practice for this presentation in front of peers throughout the year.

Website Portfolio

Perhaps the most interesting, fruitful, and problematic issue in assessment today is the movement onto the World Wide Web. Numerous possibilities arise when a portfolio becomes both digital and easily accessible. A wide variety of portfolios are currently being placed on websites, with most being what we might call exhibition portfolios. Many of these are actually small displays of selected student work created by the teacher, although some are actually more extensive and student-controlled. (e.g. http://www.mehs.educ.state.ak.us/portfolios/portfolio.html

In our discussions, we have thought extensively about the construction of web-based portfolios because this is an area in which the potentials are enormous for facilitating assessment dialogues and interaction. One aspect of the process that we feel merits more attention is that these  digital portfolios need to exist on several levels. As with a print portfolio, the sampling portfolio would serve as a depository for student selected samples of their work, including multiple drafts and revisions. There should be several copies of this: one on a classroom hard drive or school intranet and one that the student stores on a zip disk, external drive, or CD-ROM.

In line with our vision of assessment as a partnership, we advocate a second level of the digital portfolio that encompasses all of the assessment tools used and compiles these into a internet-based portfolio. From the extensive sampling portfolio managed by the student, the student and teacher would select evidence of the student's progress and make connections to rubrics, narratives, goals, reflections, and other assessment materials valued by the school. This internet-based portfolio would be more polished, more selective, and more interactive, with the teacher dialoguing and reacting to student's work. There would also be peer feedback and self-evaluation at this level. Copies of this digitized report could be kept on file at the school and sent home to parents, used in conferences with parents or caregivers, and even sent to colleges in lieu of report cards. Depending on the learning community, the digital portfolio may include grades, checklists, standard rubrics, and graphs, as well as anecdotal observations by teachers. This digital-based portfolio could be available online, but if so it would be essential that these materials be secure and accessible only with a password. There are certainly benefits to parents having ready access to the full range of assessment materials, but there are also issues of security. If anything is to be exhibited is probably more beneficial to add another more selective layer to the reporting process.

Figure 7-3. Levels of the Web-Based Portfolio Process

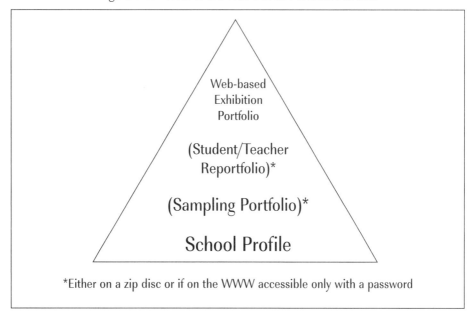

Web-based
Exhibition
Portfolio

(Student/Teacher
Reportfolio)*

(Sampling Portfolio)*

School Profile

*Either on a zip disc or if on the WWW accessible only with a password

The final level, the exhibition portfolio, can be accessible on-line and essentially student controlled. This is the most selective level of the process and might be used quite effectively for presentations and exhibits, during student-led conferences, and to open learning and assessment up to the wider community.

An effective set-up of the web-based portfolio might include a school profile page with the following:

- An explanation of the philosophy and the system of assessment

- Instructions or help page, with a link to this available throughout

- Base page with brief introduction, list of students, and links to individual student pages

Student pages might contain:

- Links to project and work sample pages

- Links to project goals, assignment (context for project), early drafts, journal entries, and related projects

- Links to teacher evaluations (grade with criteria, rubric, narratives, etc.), peer or self-evaluations, and reaction from parents, community, and other audiences

- Chatroom or discussion board where parents, teachers, and students could communicate about assessment practices.

There are issues related both to placing student materials online and opening up online dialogue to students. It is important to carefully consider what is appropriate to place on student pages if they are made accessible to the public. More importantly, teachers should discuss what is appropriate with students, in terms of both the information they will place in their exhibition portfolios (for example, will photographs or last names of students be included?) and general online safety. Students should be aware that a stranger is a stranger whether they approach you on the sidewalk or on the internet.

Potential Problems

- Websites are vulnerable to outsiders; teachers may not want them commenting on work or even visiting the site.

- The school needs its own server or an agreement with a company that offers this type of service. In addition, schools need enough hardware and software for all students to be able to make their own web-based portfolios, including scanners, computers with web-authoring and graphics software, and digital cameras, among other needs.

- The school needs to provide training and support for teachers and for students. Training for parents and caregivers would also be beneficial.

- In order to interact, parents would need to be connected to the web or have some access to a computer such as at a public library or at work.

Reflecting on Digital Assessments

The recent technological revolution has created a situation in which students are often more competent at learning how to use software and hardware than their teachers. Coupled with this is the fact that students often find using computers to be rewarding. Because of student competence and the opportunity for teaching the teachers and parents that accompanies this, as well as student interest in technology, digital assessments are a natural means of engaging students in the process of reflecting their learning. Technology is changing rapidly; using technology for assessment places students in the position of developing the skills and, more important, the attitudes of lifelong learners. While teachers may hesitate to incorporate technology into their assessment processes, they may find that doing so will increase student motivation. Finally, digital assessment tools allow students and teachers to represent learning through multiple means—language, visual items, and sound. This flexibility allows a richer representation of what a student can do across a range of activities.

Part III

Assessment Conversations

Eight

Parent–Teacher Conferences

Introduction

The next two chapters offer a continuum of conferencing possibilities. This chapter presents a child-centered approach to the traditional parent-teacher conference, as well as conference formats that focus primarily on conversations between parents and teacher but that also involve students. The next chapter extends the continuum to student-led conferences in which students set the agenda and lead the conversation. Conferences provide all stakeholders with an occasion to consider work samples and written assessment materials such as portfolios, dossiers, and web pages and to converse about those materials. Conferences establish important relationships between parents, teachers, and students. They are the site of planning for the future, presenting and reviewing educational goals, solving problems, and creating connections between a student's life at school and life at home.

Parent-teacher conferences offer opportunities for parents to converse with teachers about their child. It is time for parents to hear not only how their child is doing academically and socially but how they, as parents, can become partners in their child's educational program.

Assessment as a Partnership

Parent-teacher conferences provide an opportunity for parents and teachers to share insights into the social, academic, and physical development of the child. This is a golden opportunity for ongoing communication and planning since parents play a vital role in their child's learning. Conferencing can provide an avenue for teachers and parents to view children through different lenses and perspectives. By sharing what each knows about the student, each can better direct current and future learning. Through this collaboration, both the parent and teacher can assess the student's work and formulate realistic goals for themselves and the student.

Teachers should encourage and nurture the relationship with parents. Ways this can be done include frequent and ongoing conversations with the parent via telephone calls, classroom newsletters, and parent letters. These conversations need to be positive and uplifting. Parents too often only receive feedback from the teacher when there is a problem, thus creating a one-way communication system with the home. We see a need for frequent and ongoing conversations that highlight and reinforce what the child can do.

What information do parents need to know during these conferences? Many parents want to know how their child is doing in class—both academically and socially. They are eager to learn about particular patterns of learning, growth, and progress that have taken place over time.

Focus on the Student: Work Samples

During our conversations with teachers about the procedures they followed when conducting parent-teacher conferences, we learned that many of the teachers used work samples—completed work and works in progress—to focus on the child's learning patterns. Teachers frequently used portfolios and folders as a way to manage and store student work samples.

Two of the teachers we observed believed that teaching and learning begins with the philosophy that students are active learners and that they have a voice in their learning. These teachers encourage their students to reflect upon their learning and clarify their thoughts through written reflection and discussion. Tammy, a fourth-grade teacher, used folders as a way to document student learning over time. She shared that "by placing student work in special folders, the students learn that their work is important and valued. My students are constantly thinking and making decisions about their work." Another teacher, Barbara, who taught third grade, preferred using portfolios. She stated that "what the students put into their portfolios isn't what is important, but what counts is they are thinking and talking about their work accountability." Portfolios of student-selected and self-evaluated work bring the student's voice into the parent-teacher conference.

Phases of the Parent-Teacher Conferences

The primary purpose of the parent-teacher conference is to focus on the child while building a partnership between the parent and teacher.

Sitting at a table, the parents and the teacher look through the student's work together. Since the teacher has met individually with the child and reviewed the work samples, the teacher should have a good understanding of the child's current level of performance and the progress made during the grading term. This information can then be shared with the parent. It is at this time that the parent can provide additional information or extend the information that is shared. This is an opportunity for both the parent and teacher to speak openly and honestly about the child's progress while addressing concerns. This is also the time at which both the teacher and parent may learn all they can about the child in order to continue to provide support, encouragement, and reinforcement.

Although there are many ways to prepare for a parent-teacher conference, we recommend that teachers consider four key phases when planning and preparing for the conference. These include gathering evidence, looking at the evidence, arriving at conclusions, and setting goals as demonstrated (Figure 8-1). It is important that all stakeholders (student, teacher, and parent) are active participants throughout each of the four phases even if the student is not present at the conference.

Selecting materials for the conference can be completed by the child or in collaboration with the teacher. In both instances, time is needed to review completed projects as well as works "in progress." After materials are selected, the student needs to evaluate his learning through reflection and self-evaluation. This is typically completed through a written response attached to the selected piece. Students can opt to share their reflections with peers prior to scheduling a conference with the teacher. It is during this teacher-student conference that the student will share what he or she has chosen and written along with a guide sheet that the teacher will share with the parents. This guide sheet, as shown below, depicts the student's thoughts and reflections about his or her learning in the areas of academics, social skills, and work habits. This guide sheet can serve as a conversation starter between the teacher and parent in the absence of the student.

Student guide sheet for parent-teacher conferences

Yes—Sometimes—No

Goals for term

I wanted to a better planner (think ahead, ask my questions)

Research topics using different materials

Try different organizations of ideas

Use web sites as a resource

Work with and help partners

Make interesting presentations and projects

Make more contributions during class discussions

Build upon my classmates ideas

Work Habits

I used my time wisely

I had materials available and ready

Volunteer support and input to others

I have made the most improvement in

I still need to work on . . .

My parents can support me at home by . . .

Parent-Teacher Conference Formats

There are many ways to set up a parent-teacher conference. As you explore the many possibilities, keep in mind that all of the formats have advantages and that the format you implement must fit into your particular situation, teaching style, and purpose. The three most frequently used conference formats, as shown in Figure 8-2, are the traditional parent-teacher conference, the parent-teacher conference with child present, and the parent-teacher conference with input from the child.

Format 1: Traditional Parent-Teacher Conference

In this format, the student is typically not invited to the conference and the teacher and parent meet to discuss student growth and progress. The student is still encouraged to select the materials that will be shared and to complete the student guide sheet illustrated above.

The benefits of using this format include an opportunity for parent and teacher to converse openly about the child's learning. This is also a time when the parent and the teacher can raise sensitive issues regarding the child's academic or social learning. The factors to consider when using this format might include the student becoming anxious about the things that might be shared in his or her absence.

Figure 8-1. Phases of Parent-Teacher Conferences

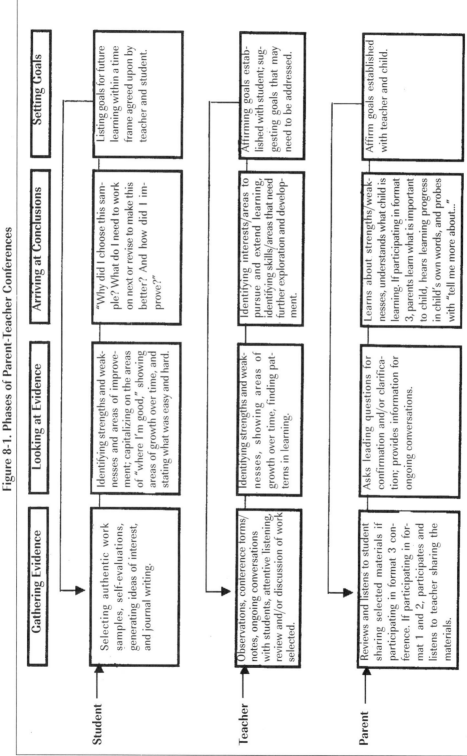

Format 2: Parent-Teacher Conference With Child Present

This format enables the student to be present at the conference and to listen to what is being shared about his or her growth and progress. The student will still complete the student guide sheet and select the materials that will be shared.

The benefits of this format include the student having the opportunity to listen and offer input to the conversation between the teacher and parent. The disadvantage is that the student may be only listening. The factors to consider when implementing this format could be that the parent and teacher might need to be guarded about what is being discussed. It may also be very difficult for the child to remain silent while work is being shared and discussed.

Format 3: Parent-Teacher Conference With Input From the Student

This format has two parts. During the first part, the child, teacher, and parent sit together and the student shares the work that was selected. After the student shares the work samples, the student leaves the room and the parent and teacher continue the conference.

The benefits of this format include open communication between all stakeholders (student, parent, and teacher) at the onset of the conference. The parent has an opportunity to hear how their child is doing from the child's perspective. The factors to consider include preplanning supervised activities for the child after he or she leaves the conference. Attention and care must be made to the type of activities planned in order to minimize the distractions to others.

Figure 8-2. Parent-Teacher Conference Formats

Type of Conferences	Description	Benefits	Factors to Consider
Format 1: Traditional Parent-Teacher Conference	Parent and teacher meet to discuss student growth and progress. Student is typically not invited to attend.	Open conversations between teacher and parent, sensitive issues can be raised and discussed.	Student not involved in conference, thus input from student. Child may become anxious about what is being said in his/her absence.
Format 2: Parent-Teacher Conference With Child present	Parent and teacher meet to discuss student growth and progress. Student is invited to attend and listen to what is being discussed.	The student is able to hear the discussion between the teacher and parent.	Both teacher and parent are guarded by what is being discussed.
Format 3: Parent-Teacher Converence With Input From the Student	The student begins the conference by sharing work samples that have been selected. Student then leaves the conference so the teacher and parent can continue conference.	Open communication between all stakeholders— student, parent, teacher. Parent can hear how child is doing from child's perspective.	Organization and preplanning of supervised activity for the students after leaving the conference. Some type of transition system in place to minimize distractions to others.

Preparing for Parent-Teacher Conferences

There are many ways teachers can prepare for parent-teacher conferences. As shown in Figure 8-3, there are specific roles and responsibilities that each stakeholder (i.e., student, teacher, and parent) assumes when preparing for these conferences. Depending on the format selected, the role of the student differs dramatically. For instance, if the student will not be present at the conference, then his or her only role is to select the material to be shared and write a self-evaluation. In contrast, if the student will be present and sharing work samples (formats 2 and 3), then he or she is responsible for preparing the materials and sharing them with the parents. Even though the student does not direct the conference, he or she is able to respond to the comments made by either the teacher or parent. The teacher's role during the conference is to encourage discussion. Regardless of the format selected, the focus of the conference remains on the child and his or her progress and goals.

Although Barbara and Tammy conduct a more traditional parent-teacher conference (similar to format 1), they implement a child-centered approach to preparing for conferences by meeting individually with all of their students prior to the conference. Barbara shared the following,

> I gain insights about my students by reading their brief phrases or noticing how they view their work. I start asking questions, and I have learned to wait for a response. I am amazed that when the parents come

in for their conference, many are fascinated with their child's self-evaluations—they want to know how their child thinks he or she is doing and what he or she thinks his or her strengths and weaknesses are. [I know this] does take time, but it is worth it.

Figure 8-3. Preparing for Parent-Teacher Conferences: Roles and Responsibilities

Student	Writes invitation for open-house/parent curriculum night, sets goals, selects work to be shared, writes reflection/reactions to work selected, writes invitation to parents and guardians.	Format 1: student not present; Format 2: student is listener and observer; Format 3: student proceeds with conference and shares work samples, journals, and center activities. Student engages parents in conversation and shares progress.	In formats 1 and 2, the student reviews the portfolio with parents at home. In format 3 the student reflects on the conference and completes evaluation form.
Teacher	Explains to parents the philosophy and procedures of classroom during open-house/ parent curriculum night; assists in setting goals, collects work samples.	The teacher's role will depend on the conference format selected. In addition to the specified roles within each format, the teacher will facilitate the conference by providing appropriate support and encouragement.	Reflects on current instructional practices and finds alternative ways to scaffold learning and affirm goals.
Parent	Respond to child's invitation to both open-house/parent curriculum night and conference data; listens and asks question of teacher and/ or student (depending on format); begins thinking about goals that could be considered.	Focus on child's work, listen and give appropriate feedback to either teacher and/or child (depending on format); ask probing questions for further detail during the conference; initiate conversation pertaining to concerns or issues about child's progress.	Suggest and add goals, complete feedback for classroom teacher and write letter to child.

Both Barbara and Tammy provide a structured schedule that students adhere to when planning and preparing for these conferences (Table 8-1). As students select materials to be shared, they also participate in self-assessments that include completing a bar graph to illustrate their growth and progress. When completing this graph, students are asked to mark their current status and their expected level of progress. They also participate in portfolio sharing with a peer. At the completion of this activity, the peer provides written feedback.

Table 8-1: Preparing for the Parent-Teacher Conference

Procedures/Steps	Barbara	Tammy – 4th Grade
Collection of Student Work	Called a "portfolio."	Called a "collection of work" folder.
Review process	Individual students peruse portfolio and select work to be shared at conference. Students complete self-assessments.	Individual students peruse work folder and select work to be shared at conference. Students complete self-assessments.
Student Self-Assessment	Individual students assess learning by responding to specific questions and completing a graph.	Individual students assess learning by responding to specific questions and completing a graph.
Conferencing With Student	Student completes graph, self-assessment, and portfolio before coming to teacher conference. Teacher reviews work samples with students. Teacher asks probing questions to get as much information from student as possible. This conference is usually 30 minutes.	Student completes graph and self-assessment before coming to teacher conference. Teacher reviews work sample with all students.
Report Cards	Teacher completes district report card form.	Teacher completes district report card form.

About a week prior to the conference, both Tammy and Barbara meet with each student. Together they review the portfolio or work folder and set goals for the next grading term. Barbara then sends the portfolios home with the goal sheet attached. With their parents, the students review the portfolio and goal sheet and the parents are asked what concerns and issues they would like to have addressed at the parent-teacher conference. After the parent has had an opportunity to review the portfolio and discuss the contents with their child, the portfolio and response sheet are returned to school.

During and After the Conference

Table 8-2 illustrates the procedures Tammy and Barbara follow when conducting conferences. They encourage conversation and reinforce what the student is able to do. They begin the conference with a brief review of the school-wide documents, leaving most of the time allotted for discussion and sharing of the student work and reflections. The completed student's guide sheet (discussed earlier in this chapter) is shared also with the work samples. The parents are then asked to complete a comment form at the close of the conference.

Table 8-2: During and After Parent-Teacher Conference

Procedures/Steps	Barbara – 3rd Grade	Tammy – 4th Grade
Time Allotted Review Documents Review Student Documents	30 minutes Current report card. Review student work samples, student self-assessment, and graph.	30 minutes Current report card. Review student work samples, student self-assessment, and graph.
Interactions Between Teacher and Parent	Both parents and teacher review the collection of student's work samples.	Parents can take materials home after conference. Both parents and teacher review the collection of student's work samples. The materials stay in the classroom and are returned to the work folder after the conference.
Feedback	Parents complete a response or comment form.	Parents complete a response or comment form.

Many teachers have a collection of the child's work from several subject areas showing a progression of skill development. One popular method teachers frequently use is called Monday folders. This method enables students to take home the folder that contains work from the previous week. The weekly encounter with the Monday folder encourages parents to sit down with their child at home to review the work, engage in conversations, and to assess learning and progress over time. The students have the option to select anything from their Monday folder to put into their portfolios. By doing so, students have an opportunity to assess their work frequently and to choose work samples that can be shared at the parent-teacher conference.

Reactions to Parent–Teacher Conferences

We have spent considerable time interviewing students and their parents about such conferences and found general support for the activities. Most parents who engage in parent-teacher conferences believe that they afford an opportunity to learn about their child in a focussed, supportive, and celebratory fashion. They appreciate their child's involvement in school activities. Most of the students, however, would prefer to participate in the discussion rather than being informed by the teacher or their parent as to their progress. Here is a sample of the comments that we heard:

Cynthia: Could you share your thoughts about the advantages of parent-teacher conferences?

Parent #1:   I try to learn all I can about each of my children. I want to know how each one is developing socially, emotionally, and academically. I like to zero in on each subject as well. Their teacher's perspective gives me a framework. I try to figure out how I can best support each of my children so they can develop to their fullest potential in all areas. I wish that more conferences were held, but I realize how time-consuming it is for teachers. Sometimes, teachers opt not to conference with me at all. They say that a conference is unnecessary because my child is progressing beautifully in all areas. I still like to meet with the teacher and review work samples together. I learn from her observations and hopefully she learns from mine.

Child #1: I don't like parent-teacher conferences that much because I want to know what they say about me. Just having my mom come home and tell me that my teacher said, "She's doing fine" doesn't tell me much.

Parent #2: In a student-led conference, I think you get more of what the child is doing in the classroom because they are showing you their work in the different areas. In the teacher-led conference, you can focus more on some of the questions you might have on how your child is doing that you would not necessarily ask with them there. I think there are pros and cons to both.

Cynthia: Could you elaborate more on what you think are the pros and cons of both kinds of conferences?

Parent #2: If you have questions/concerns that you didn't want to broach with your child beside you, it's easier in a teacher-led conference. But, I think if you have that kind of situation, I would think you could always request a conference on your own. At least, this way (in a student-led conference), your child is getting your full undivided attention as to what they're learning in school.

Parent #3: I think the kids open up more [with a student-led conference]. I mean, they're telling you their feelings and their side of what they've done. I think it's just better having your child there. It's nice to have both there so they can explain things to you.

Reflections on Parent–Teacher Conferences

We all have a stake in the growth of our students; other than of the students themselves, parents are the ones with the longest term and most serious stake in their children's growth. Parents may or may not have a lot of information about pedagogy or education themselves, but they have concerns that need to be heard. The parent-teacher conference is a place for everyone who cares about a child to communicate that care and the desire for that child to grow in the best way possible. It is a place to solve problems and to create correspondences and consistency between school and home expectations. Through self-evaluation and through students' selection of their own work for the conference portfolio, students' voices can also become part of the conversation. The result is that the education a child receives is tailored to his or her needs and that teachers and parents learn from each other in the interest of supporting a child's growth.

Nine

Student-Led Conferencing

Introduction

Conferencing with parents is a natural extension of assessing students. Traditionally, parent-teacher conferences are held to supplement ongoing observations, anecdotal documentation, and report cards. Conferences provide the opportunity for parents and teachers to meet and discuss a child's progress. The child's social and academic strengths and weaknesses are discussed, allowing parents and teachers to gain new perspectives. Many teachers have invited the students, who are eager to participate, to the conferences to remove the mystery that surrounds such conversations. As one fifth-grade student interviewed explained, "I want to be there so that I can hear what the teacher thinks my strengths and weakness are and not just to be told from my parents when they get home that I'm doing okay."

As described in the above scenario, another way to assess and inform parents about the learning progress is through student-led conferences. These conferences shift the focus from teacher as informant to student as informant. When participating in a student-led conference, the emphasis is not only on academic content but also on social relationships, student self-evaluations, and personal and academic goals that the student feels are important in his or her learning. Conferences provide an opportunity for the student to take an active role in the assessment process as well as for the teacher and parent to view learning from a student's perspective.

Student-led conferences provide opportunities for students to show their teachers and parents what they are thinking and how they are learning. This style of conferencing promotes self-reflection, goal setting, and responsibility. As the student conducts the conference, the teacher leads from behind, providing support and encouragement when needed, enabling students to internalize essential skills that will be valued throughout life. Preparing for and leading the conference allows students to engage in conversations with teachers, parents, and peers, thus enabling them to reflect upon their learning, demonstrate their ability to articulate strengths and weaknesses, and provide insights about their learning patterns and strategies.

Phases of the Student-Led Conference

From our observations and conversations with teachers, we have identified four phases pertaining to student-led conferences. These include:

- Gathering evidence of what they have done or might do

- Developing ways to look at evidence for the purpose of drawing conclusions

- Arriving at conclusions regarding accomplishments, goals, and important areas of interest

- Setting goals

These goals should be both short- and long-term. The stakeholders (e.g., student, parent, and teacher) take an active role in all four phases, as illustrated in Figure 9-1.

Student-led conferences reflect the ways in which learning takes place in the classroom. The child has responsibility for his or her learning. Parents, the student, and the teacher have the opportunity to look at the same piece of work. Areas of growth and development are discussed. Parents actively participate and share their ideas about learning possibilities and strengths and can seek clarification on why a particular piece was selected. The child can explain the thinking that went into the work. As they discuss each piece, depth of understanding emerges. The parents and teacher are encouraged to ask questions and give feedback concerning the child's learning. With all parties present, facts are less likely to be distorted. If discrepancies arise, this group can solve the problems together. Thus, this type of conference reflects a collaborative effort among all stakeholders.

As we observed several student-led conferences, we were impressed with the level of reflection students demonstrated when discussing their work with their teacher and parents. In a second-grade classroom, a boy was sharing his gathering folder with his mother. The materials included a letter to his mother about a meal he would like her to make and why the foods he selected were nutritious, a story he had written about observing seeds and plants, his science prediction and tests about the movement of a pendulum, and a couple of mathematics assignments on estimation and problem solving. He opened the conference by explaining how he solved the mathematics problem using particular problem-

Figure 9-1. Phases of Student-Led Conferences

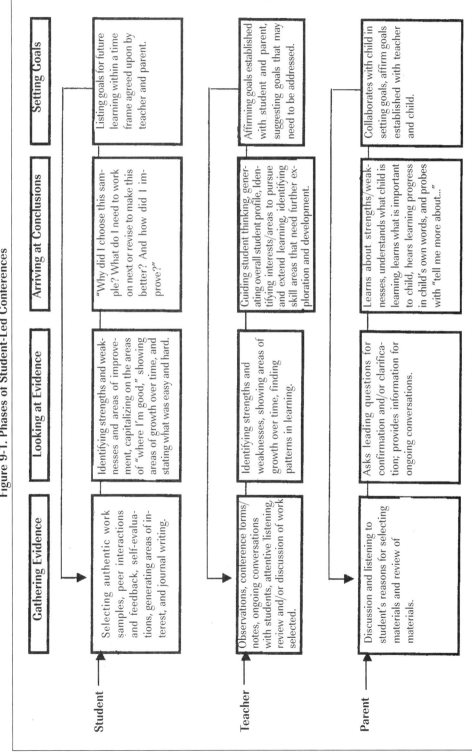

solving and estimation techniques. He explained that his technique was "estimating the multidigit numbers to the nearest tens." His second selection was a paper he wrote about plants and seeds.

Child: I like this piece because I really put some good words in it. It's about seeds, and I wrote about growing and all of that.

Parent: Did you write what you saw?

Child: Yeah. I like this because I wrote a lot of descriptive words.

He then shared the science experiment he had completed that morning. He showed how he made the pendulum out of weights, string, and a ruler. While describing to his mother how he made it, the teacher joined the conference. When he finished his explanation, the teacher asked him to read his prediction and to explain the steps he followed when he conducted the experiment earlier that day.

Child: I predicted that the heavier it is, the slower it will go. The less heavy, the faster it will go.

Teacher: How did you come up with that prediction?

Child: We did the experiment using those (pointing to the other pendulums taped on the front of the board).

Components of a Student-Led Conference

We observed a number of different items being shared during student-led conferences:

- Portfolios (e.g., working or showcase)
- Completed assignments in content area subjects (for older grades) or thematic unit projects (younger grades)
- Inventories
- Self-evaluations or assessments
- Current reading books
- Journals or learning logs
- Writing samples (e.g., poems, research reports, letters, predictions, reflections, stories)
- Goal-setting forms

Although the materials shared in each of the conferences were consistent, the reasons the materials were selected and the procedures students followed when conducting their conferences were unique. For example, in middle and high school, students typically selected the following items:

- At least two work samples (a good and a bad example) from each content area
- One entry from their social studies journal

- One or two tests from at least one subject area
- One science project
- Copies of two questionnaires that asked open-ended questions about their personal feelings in particular situations and about their study habits
- Their goals for the upcoming term

As students shared, it became evident that the work samples reflected high percentages or grades. Further, the goals established by middle or high school students included improving time management and listing ways that would help them maintain their high grades. As one student shared, "I am very well organized, and I want to have more time to get to class, so if I go to my locker once in the morning I can get to class on time." Additionally, many students used technology such as computers to write their goals.

In the elementary grades, student-led conferences often emphasized portfolios. At several of the sites, students shared a working portfolio that contained work samples in progress and ongoing projects. Students selected a few examples from this portfolio to share with time allotted for parents to browse through the materials not selected. One classroom used the term *gathering folder*, representing all the work completed during a grading period. A new gathering folder would be established at the beginning of each new term. The work samples not selected for the portfolio would remain in the gathering folder and would be sent home at mid-term with the portfolio for the student and parent to review. All gathering folders would be included in the portfolio and would be sent home at the end of the school year.

A student's showcase portfolio was often shared with parents during conferences if the student wanted to compare work samples to demonstrate growth over time. We observed this type of comparison during a visit to a second-grade classroom. The student was sharing selected pieces—a reading book, a written story, a classroom book, pen pal letters, mathematics timed facts, a sample of the writing process from idea to final draft, and her journal. The student shared two writing samples, one from the beginning of the school year and the other more recent. She used this to document her learning. With both pieces she explained to her parents what she had accomplished and the process she went through from rough draft to the final copy. As she talked about the writing process, she pointed to particular areas in which she saw growth and improvement. She shared the following with her parents: "The reasons I selected these pieces are because I did pretty well. I've gotten better with punctuation since October and I wanted to improve on capitalization, kinds of words I use, and punctuation."

Setting goals is an essential component of the student-led conference.

Goal setting, like the materials shared, was accomplished in several different ways. In the older grades, students took it upon themselves to design goals that met their individual needs as a student and as a member of the school-wide community. Many of the goals defined focused on time management, socialization, and reaching higher academic status on a designated grading scale. Students identified how each goal could be achieved and the consequences if not achieved. The following is an example of a middle-school student sharing her goals with her parents:

Child: My short-term goal is to make it to class before the bell rings. I will accomplish this goal by going to my locker first thing in the morning and less often during the day. The consequence is that I'd be tardy and could miss something important. My long-term goal is to get all As and Bs for the rest of the year and to study harder for tests. I will know if I accomplish this goal by seeing As and Bs on my report card. I'll also be proud of myself and get on the merit role.

Parent: When did you set these goals?

Child: About two weeks ago.

Parent: How are you doing so far?

Child: Okay.

For upper elementary students, goals emphasized working harder, reading more books of different genres, completing assignments, understanding mathematics concepts (mathematics facts, division, decimals, and fractions), and focusing on skill areas in writing such as spelling, word choice, punctuation, and capitalization. For lower elementary students, the goals designed by students typically included reading more books, reading harder books, writing more stories, writing more neatly, adding and subtracting bigger numbers, and working harder on mathematics. The forms we found in these classrooms differed by grade and teacher. For the older students, the goals were typically typed out in list form and shared at the conference. For many of the upper elementary students, goals were written on index cards that were read and shared at the conference. The younger students were provided forms to complete either individually or with the assistance of the teacher.

In one conference, we listened as a lower elementary student shared her goals with her parents: "I like writing but I need to write more poems. I love to read, but I need to read more AER books [leveled books that are entered into the computer for competency testing]. I just love to talk, but I need to do more projects in front of the class." Another student from the same class not only shared her goals with her father but also spent several minutes reflecting upon her learning strengths and weakness in each curriculum area as she shared her goals.

The teacher at one site led the goal-setting meeting after the student-led conference. The teacher was not part of the student-led conference but sat at a table away from the conference. As students completed the conference with their parents, they moved to the teacher's table where the teacher facilitated the goal-setting aspect of the conference. As the student, parents, and teacher sat together, the teacher served as scribe and directed probing questions to both the student and parents. She opened the conference by asking the student what he or she wanted to focus on during the upcoming term. After recording the students' comments, she turned to the parents and asked them to share their ideas and recommendations. The teacher also encouraged parents to establish goals that could be linked to home in order to form a stronger relationship between the home and school. The teacher then shared her observations, insights, and thoughts as to where the student "could go from here" by discussing ideas she had on what approach she would take in planning instruction for this student. In this collaborative exchange and planning meeting, broad concepts and a "road map" were sketched out regarding what activities and learning goals the student, teacher, and parent would participate in during the upcoming term.

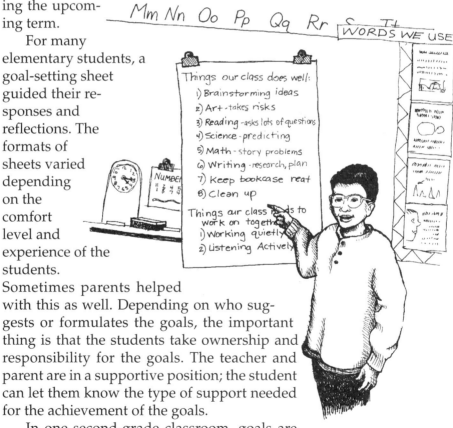

For many elementary students, a goal-setting sheet guided their responses and reflections. The formats of sheets varied depending on the comfort level and experience of the students. Sometimes parents helped with this as well. Depending on who suggests or formulates the goals, the important thing is that the students take ownership and responsibility for the goals. The teacher and parent are in a supportive position; the student can let them know the type of support needed for the achievement of the goals.

In one second-grade classroom, goals are written at the beginning of each grading term. The goals are reviewed twice each term, once at the mid-term break and again when report cards are distributed. As each term comes to a close, the students review their goals, comment on the progress or completion of each goal, and then set new goals for the upcoming term. For the fall term, the students in this classroom were to write three goals that related to home, school, and community. At the end of the first grading term, Katherine reviewed and reflected on three goals she had established earlier in the term. Figure 9-2 illustrates Katherine's goals for the first grading term. Her reflections were written under the category "What did I do?" Her goal for school, "to read books more," was achieved since she wrote, "I reached my goal because I read more books." For home Katherine wanted "to do my homework right when I get home." She is well on her way to achieving this goal since she wrote "I reached my goal a little bit because I'm starting to do my homework right when I get home." For her third goal, community, Katherine wanted to participate in Christmas caroling. She wrote, "I reached my goal because I went in girl scouts."

For second term, Katherine wanted to focus on reading and language arts. Figure 9-3 depicts the goals she established. (Student's original spelling has been maintained.) After completing the goals, she scheduled a goal conference with her teacher to discuss the goals she created. For reading she wrote, "I want to improve on reading more books because I'm not reading very much." For writing, Katherine stated, "I'm good at writing because I try to write neater." She wanted to work on her oral speaking skills for the upcoming term. She wrote, "I am not a good speaker because I am shy." She felt her strength lay in listening "because I don't bother my neighbor." It is likely that this goal would be discussed at length during the conference since it is more of an observation than a goal. Katherine's teacher will most likely ask her parents to help elaborate on writing, speaking, and listening goals in order to incorporate areas that Katherine could emphasize during the winter term. The teacher might also encourage a goal that will reinforce what her parents are doing at home. For technology, Katherine would like to expand her knowledge of the keyboard and to improve her typing ability. Her goal is "I wish I could type without looking at the keys on the keyboard." This goal could certainly extend to the home environment where her parents could assist in her learning.

For the third term, Katherine wrote three goals that emphasized reading, mathematics, and class discussions. The goal she established for mathematics was "I could practice math more and challenge myself in math." For reading, she wrote, "I could read more books; and for class discussions she wrote, "I could answer more questions in class." Figures 9-4 and 9-5 illustrate her third-term goals and her reflections on the progress of these goals. During the third term, students have the opportunity to establish goals that will be shared with parents at the end of the term.

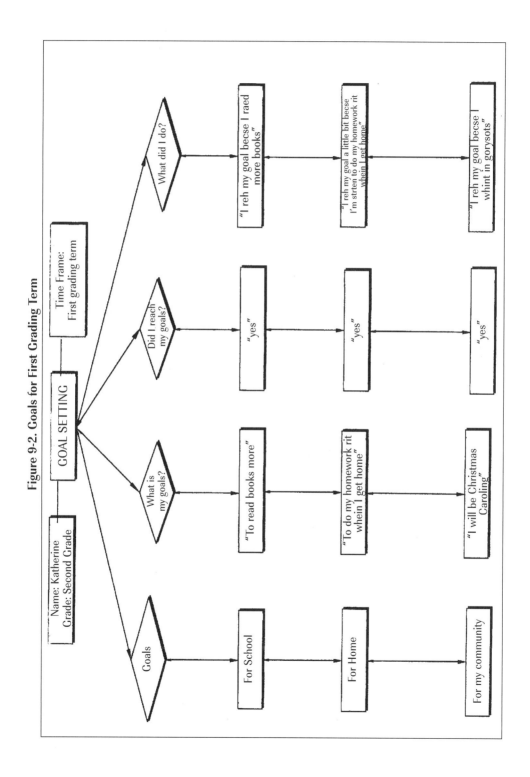

Figure 9-2. Goals for First Grading Term

Figure 9-3. Goals for Second Grading Term

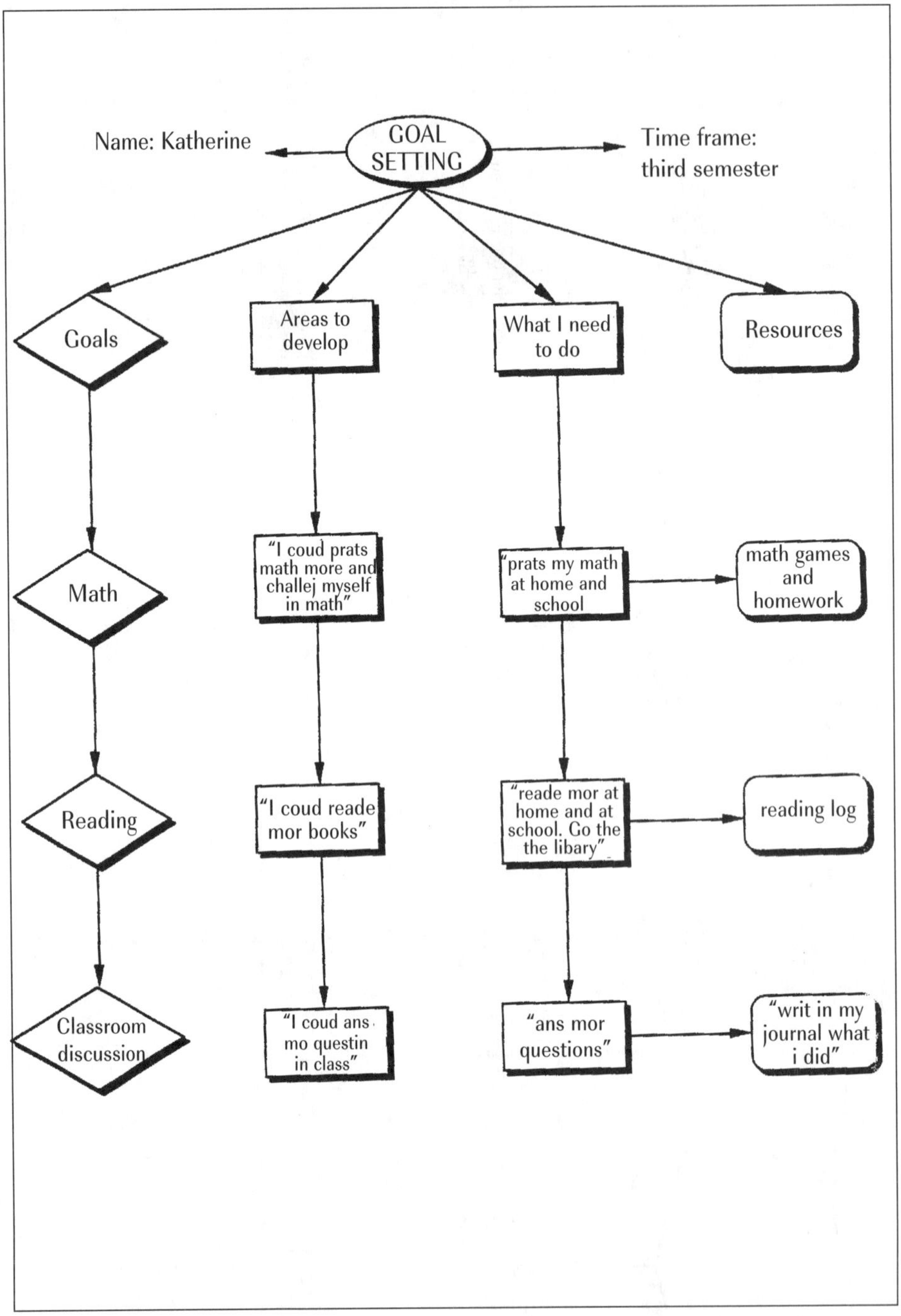

Figure 9-4. Katherine's Goals for Reading and Language Arts
Winter Term/Grade 2

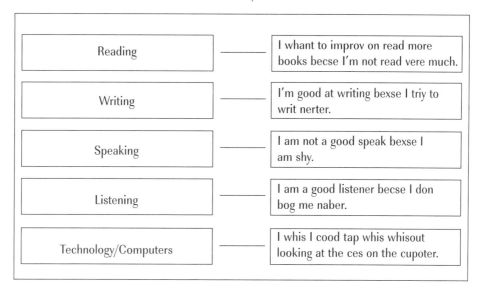

Reading	———	I whant to improv on read more books becse I'm not read vere much.
Writing	———	I'm good at writing bexse I triy to writ nerter.
Speaking	———	I am not a good speak bexse I am shy.
Listening	———	I am a good listener becse I don bog me naber.
Technology/Computers	———	I whis I cood tap whis whisout looking at the ces on the cupoter.

During a visit to Katherine's classroom, we talked with several students preparing for their spring student-led conferences. Carrie, a cheerful, confident child, was sitting at her desk completing her goals for the upcoming conference. As we watched her work, we asked if she would mind sharing what she was writing. She did not mind talking to us, but she kept her attention on her work and wrote as she talked. She shared that she was looking over the goals she had previously made, needed to write a reflection on her progress, and then make new goals. She mentioned that she had three goals for the first term, two for the second term, and she was in the process of making goals for the next term. She showed us the goals and reflections she had made for the first term. Her goal for school was "to write at least 10 books." Her reflection indicates that she achieved this goal. She wrote, "Yes. I did, but some of them didn't have good detail." For home, Carrie wrote, "to be very responsible—to get a dog." She shared that she met this goal most of the time, noting that "Most of the time I was responsible but sometimes I wasn't that responsible." Her third goal related to the community. She wrote, "to pick up stuff people littered." She thought she met this goal, for she wrote, "Sometimes when I walked home from school I picked up stuff on the street, on the sidewalk, and in the grass. But sometimes there wasn't any litter to pick up."

For the second term, Carrie chose two goals related to writing. Her first goal was "practicing punctuation." Her reflection on this goal is as follows: "Yes. I wrote more stories like when I wrote when I went to the Columbus Zoo and when I learned to tie my shoe. I even wrote a poem called birds!" Her second goal was "creating new ideas." She also met

Figure 9-5. Reflections on Goals

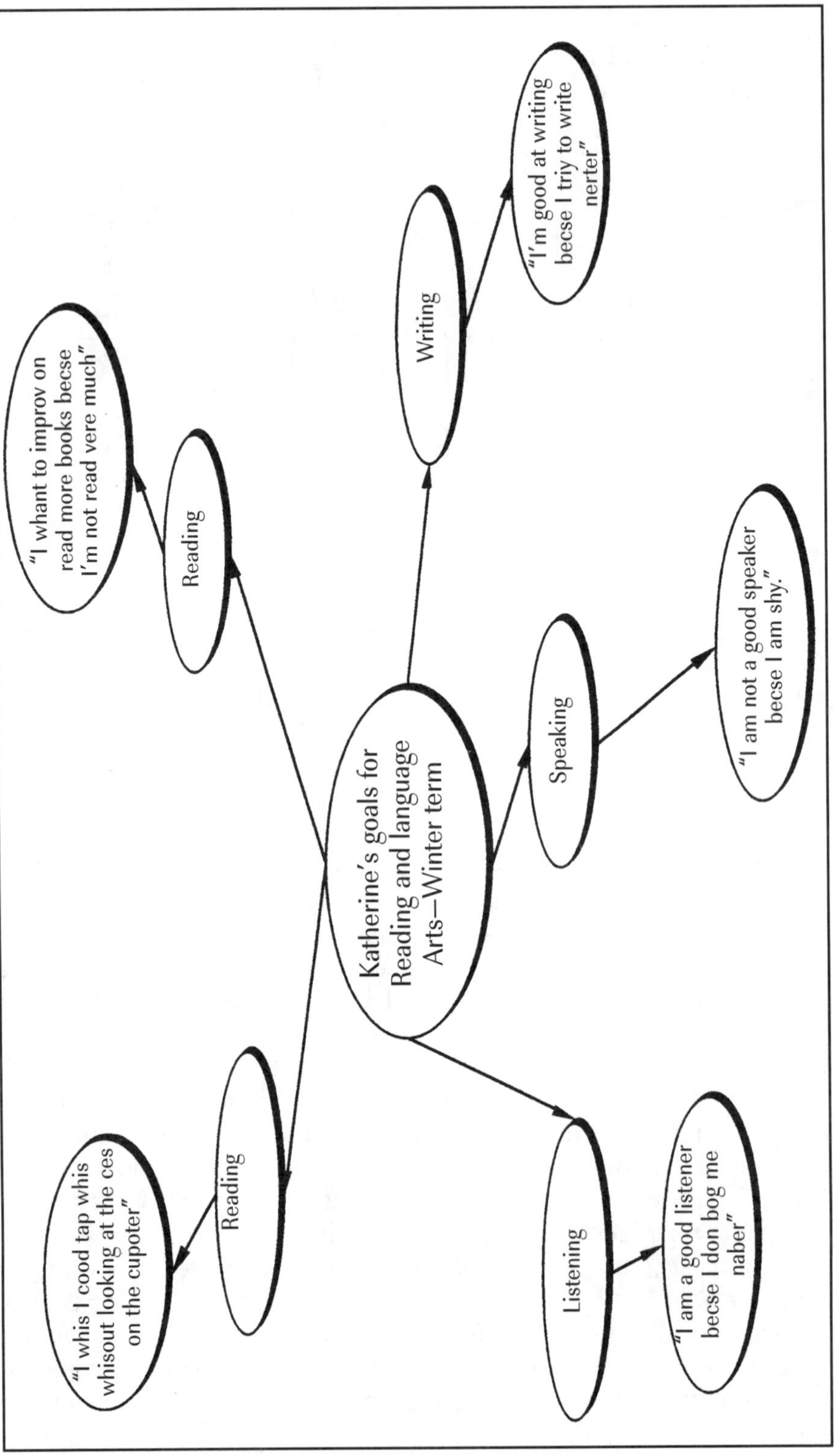

"I whant to improv on read more books becse I'm not read vere much"

Reading

Writing

"I'm good at writing becse I triy to write nerter"

Katherine's goals for Reading and language Arts—Winter term

Speaking

"I am not a good speaker becse I am shy."

"I whis I cood tap whis whisout looking at the ces on the cupoter"

Reading

Listening

"I am a good listener becse I don bog me naber"

this goal since she wrote, "I did a crazy pop-out pattern poem and I thought of new creative ideas. At the time of our visit, Carrie was drafting new goals. She shared that her goals most likely would be: "I like writing, but I need to write more poems. I love to read, but I need to read my A.R. books [relates to the reading/computer program that the school system uses to record reading progress]. I just love to talk, but I need to do more projects in front of the class. I am good at all three of these things. I love to do all of these." Figure 9-6 depicts Carrie's first- and second-term goals and reflections.

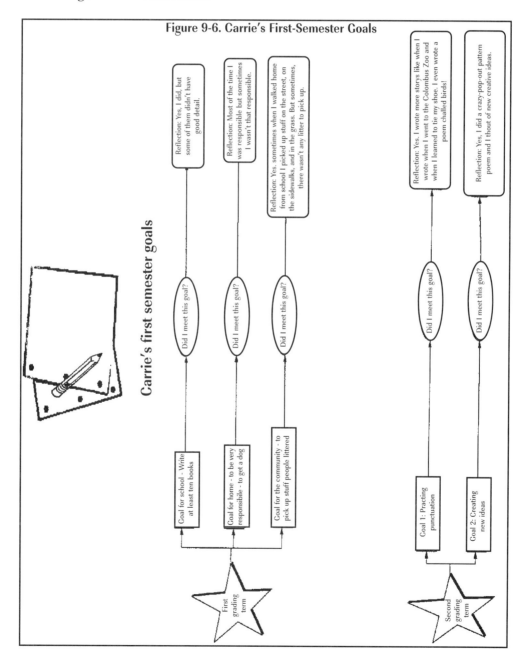

Figure 9-6. Carrie's First-Semester Goals

After observing students working in the classroom, we spoke with the classroom teacher, who shared that Carrie is a strong student who works hard and sets goals that are meaningful and purposeful to her learning and growth. She also told us that Carrie's mother, after the last student-led conference and reviewing her portfolio, wrote a letter to her daughter. In this letter, her mother praised her for work well done and identified things she would like to see Carrie attempt with the help of her teacher and herself.

Dear Carrie,

First of all, I want you to know that I am very proud of you! Learning is something that is important to me, and it makes me happy that it seems to be important to you, too. You are never too old or too smart to learn! Remember that. Here are some answers to your questions:

I noticed that you learned that you can become better at something, even if you were very good to start with. I am proud that you use your talents, try to stretch yourself, and are a good listener. Working on challenging yourself in math is something I'd like to see you do— go for it! I know you sometimes have difficulty with writing poems, but I think if you keep taking a risk, you'll be very proud of yourself. That's how you grow. I am glad to hear from Mrs. Short and Miss Jones that you follow directions. I hope you are a role model for others. I am glad to see that you are making an extra effort to always get your homework done—without ever being reminded.

I love you, and want to help you with anything you need help with. You don't always have to do everything by yourself. Keep up the good work!

Love,
XOXO
Mom

Helping Struggling Learners
Develop and Meet Goals

With students who find learning difficult, the process of developing goals may be overwhelming. It is recommended that the teacher help the student identify specific goals which they can reach but that will also stretch the student in terms of thinking and processing at the same time as they build upon their strengths.. To establish these goals, the teacher and student should work together using a strategy of thinking aloud as a way to model the steps in identifying, formulating, and drafting a goal. A teacher might say,

Let me look over what you have been doing and tell you what I have observed. Yes, you have been doing a great job of thinking about what you already know as well as finding _____ and trying _____. What do you think? Now what else might you do? What do you think? When you encounter something to wrestle with, you are _____. You seem to do _____. Are there other things you do or might do?

Once several possible goals are generated, the teacher will need to help the student limit the number of goals he or she will pursue. To select the goals, the teacher and student together could review the generated goals, prioritize them, and brainstorm possible ways each could be achieved. This information could be recorded on a chart or journal to be placed in the child's working folder for easy access and reference. The goals that were not selected could be recorded in the student's writing or reading folder or portfolio for later use.

Once the goals are selected, it is the teacher's responsibility to monitor and provide the necessary support to the student throughout the term. Follow-through is critical to progress. This support might involve the teacher conducting weekly individual conferences, documenting progress through anecdotal records, or encouraging the student to self-reflect and evaluate by charting the work completed. The teacher will want to provide an opportunity for the child to share the goals with his or her parents and elicit their support. We found that parents were more supportive of the goals when their child presented them during the student-led conference. It was at this time that the parents asked questions that encouraged the student to elaborate on the goal, give specific information regarding the steps to be taken to achieve the goal, and describe why the goals were selected. This would be a wonderful opportunity for the struggling learner to articulate specific reasons each goal was selected and to document the necessary steps or procedures he or she will take to accomplish the goal.

It is the pursuit of the goal rather than always the achievement that should be stressed; furthermore, sometimes goals change. If the student is frustrated by a perceived inability to achieve a specific goal, then the teacher might use this opportunity as a vehicle for discussion. It will be important for the teacher to approach this discussion in a positive rather than a negative way, emphasizing what was accomplished rather than what was not accomplished. It is through the review of work completed that the teacher and student can identify specific learning strategies or processes that could shed light on ways to revise the existing goal. The teacher could encourage the student to illustrate his or her learning growth through a graph or timeline as a way to document the important learning outcomes achieved.

Student-Led Conference Formats

We suggest thinking about which style makes sense in the context of classroom and teacher needs. All of these formats have advantages but the format selected needs to fit the situation, teaching style, and purpose, depending on the time of year. We found that how teachers schedule student-led conferences varied from site to site. For example, at one of the middle-school sites, the student-led conference was conducted at the semester break in January or February. A second site completed report cards twice a year, held student-led conferences in the spring, and held a parent-teacher conference in the fall. Yet another district held student-led conferences in the fall and spring and sent out narrative report cards during the other two terms. The most extensive format we found was at an elementary school where the teacher conducted two student-led conferences per year in addition to report cards. Here is her schedule:

First Term—At the end of the first 5 weeks, students select a few items from their gathering folder to be included in their showcase portfolio. For each item selected, the students respond to a question that has been generated by the class. A student-led conference is scheduled at the end of the first 10 weeks, at which the teacher helps to support students through the conference and is available for more direct involvement with parents. This preparation is especially crucial for the struggling learner. It is at this time that the teacher can provide assistance when necessary. At the end of the student-led conference, both parents and students complete a response form.

Second Term—At the end of the first 5 weeks, students again select a few items for the showcase portfolio and take home both the gathering folder and the showcase portfolio to share with parents. At the end of 20 weeks, a student-led conference is conducted at home between student and parents, with both the student and parent reflecting upon the experience through a feedback form.

Third Term—As in the second term, after the first 5 weeks students have an opportunity to select a few pieces to add to the showcase portfolios. In preparing for the mid-year conferences, students are responsible for planning and organizing their conference by practicing and conversing with peers. The classroom teacher assists only when necessary. At the end of the third term, the portfolio is sent home with grade cards.

Fourth Term—Students are encouraged to select several pieces that will go into their showcase portfolios, and their gathering folders are sent home. As during the second term, the student reviews and reflects upon the short- and long-term goals that were established throughout the year.

At the end of the year, the showcase portfolio and all four gathering folders are sent home.

The five most commonly used formats we observed are:

- Student leads and teacher prompts
- Shared conference with specific roles and responsibilities
- Student leads and teacher floats
- Student as teacher, leader, and informant
- Student selects a committee

Although we do not favor one format over another, we do strongly recommend that teachers utilize the formats that best serve their particular situation as well as providing opportunities for students to take an active role in the planning, organizing, and conducting the student-led conference.

Format 1: Student Leads and Teacher Prompts

The student, parent, and child all sit together for a 20-minute conference. The teacher opens the conference by welcoming the parents and informing them that their child will be leading the conference but that the teacher will also participate by asking questions or prompting in order for the child to provide more information. The child then begins by discussing each piece of work selected. A reflection or summary statement will be attached to each selected piece that the child may either read or refer to when sharing. Depending on the time of year, the work selected may be placed in a working or showcase portfolio. If the work is not in a portfolio, it may be placed in a large plastic bag, a colored folder, a three-ring binder, or simply be stacked in front of the student's seat. As each piece is shared, the child explains why he or she selected the piece and may comment on the degree of difficulty experienced when working on the selection. When the work samples have been shared, the child shares the goals he or she has set for the upcoming term.

The benefits of using this format include the child leading the conference and sharing the work that has been selected. There is also an opportunity for open conversations between parent, teacher, and child. The factors to consider when using this conference format include maintaining an equal amount of involvement between student and teacher, creating a balance between structured and open-ended exchanges, and being cognizant of time placed on both teachers and students when planning and implementing the conference.

Format 2: Shared Conference With Specific Roles and Responsibilities

This format has two parts: sharing of work selected and goal setting. In part one, the student and parents sit together for a 10 minute conference. Depending on the time of year, the work selected may be placed in a working or showcase portfolio. If the work is not in a portfolio, it may be placed in a large plastic bag, a colored folder, a three-ring binder, or simply be stacked in front of the student's seat. As each piece is shared, the student typically explains why he or she selected the piece and may comment on the degree of difficulty experienced when working on the selection. At the completion of the sharing session, the student and parents move to another table where the teacher joins them for the goal-setting portion of the conference. This portion also lasts for approximately 10 minutes. The teacher leads by asking probing questions and guiding the parents and students in establishing new goals for the upcoming term. The teacher serves as scribe and may also share his or her insights taken from anecdotal records or observations.

The benefits of this format include the opportunity for the child to lead an entire conference at which there is an opportunity for sustained conversations between parent and child. The child also selects and reflects upon the materials that will be shared. The factors to consider when using this format include sharing conversations with parents during the goal-setting process, sharing observations and emphasizing activities with both parent and students, and providing more time when planning and implementing.

Format 3: Student Leads While Teacher Floats

This format provides an opportunity for several conferences to be held simultaneously. The student leads the discussion about the work selected, identifying strengths and weaknesses and sharing goals he or she has established. Throughout the 20-minute conference, the teacher floats around the room and is available to parents and students to ask questions, to

listen, and to provide feedback. An important component of this format is a tour of the classroom, during which the student leads parents to particular centers in the room describing key concepts and facts he or she is learning. This is also a time where the student can participate in "reading around the room," where the child describes the daily routine of the classroom, favorite poems, charts, or written selections.

The benefits of this format include the fact that the student leads the conference and shares the work selected independently of the teacher. In addition, it is an opportunity for open communication between parent, teacher, and student. The factors to consider when using this format are sharing limited conversations with parents while drifting from conference to conference and providing more time when planning and implementing.

Format 4: Student Alone as Teacher, Leader, and Informant

This format, with the student conducting the conference with his or her parents in the absence of the teacher, has been used at all grades. The student takes complete responsibility for planning and organizing the conference and conducting the discussion regarding goals.

The benefits of using this format are that the student shares the work samples selected independently of the teacher and there is an opportunity for open and honest conversations between parent and student. Factors to consider include sharing conversations with parents independent of the teacher, accommodating the need for parents and teachers to communicate directly in such a way that does not take away from students' authority over their own work, and providing sufficient time when planning and implementing.

Format 5: Student Selects a Committee

This format has been most successful with older students, especially middle and high school students. Together, teacher and student establish the committee selection guidelines. The committee membership consists of five individuals who are selected and appointed by the student with teacher input. The committee forms at the beginning of the year and also acts as an advisory body to the student.

The benefits of this format include an excellent opportunity for the student to select individuals who will help guide and support learning and encourage collaboration and ongoing dialogue among members. Factors to consider include providing appropriate monitoring and support for social and academic development, creating flexible schedules for conferences, and maintaining open and continual communication between members.

Preparing for Student-Led Conferences

Students, parents, and teachers all take an active role in preparing for this type of conference. One of the first steps is introducing the idea to parents and students. We suggest holding a family meeting with students and parents prior to the first day of class. Alternatively, it could be incorporated into the fall open house. Some teachers have sent a letter to parents asking them to return the forms at the open house, and others have a sign-up sheet available for parents to sign that night. Figure 9-7 shows a sample letter to parents of middle school students about fall student-led conferences:

Figure 9-7. Student-Led Conference Formats

Type of Conferences	Description	Benefits	Factors to Consider
Format 1: Student leads and teacher prompts	The student leads the conference by discussing the selected pieces. As the child shares the work, the teacher prompts with questions or comments that assist the child in the description.	Child shares the work selected; child leads conference; open conversations between parent, teacher, and child.	Maintain an equal amount of involvement between student and teacher, create a balance between structured and open-ended exchanges, provide more time when planning and implementing this format.
Format 2: Shared conference with specific roles and responsibilities	Both teacher and student have a shared responsibility. The student leads parents through selected work samples. Teacher not present during initial conversations. Parents and student move to another table to set goals and discuss progress with teacher.	Child shares selected work, child leads conference, open conversations between parent and child.	Share conversations with parents during goal setting, emphasize activities with both teacher and students, provide more time when planning and implementing this format.
Format 3: Student leads and teacher floats	Several conferences are going on simultaneously in one room. The child leads the discussion, shares goals, and highlights learning strengths and areas needing improvement. Teacher floats around the room and is available to ask and answer questions.	Child is independent; child shares work selected; child leads conference; open conversation between parent, child, and teacher.	Share conversation with parents while drifting from conference to conference, provide more time when planning and implementing this format.
Format 4: Student as teacher/ leader/ informant	Conferences are conducted in the absence of teacher. Students share selected work with parents. Students lead parents through written evaluation/summary forms.	Child shares work, child is independent, opportunity for open conversation between parent and child.	Share conversation with parents while drifting from conference to conference, provide more time when planning and implementing this format.
Format 5: Student selects a committee	The committee selection guidelines are established by both students and teacher. The committee membership includes five individuals selected by the student with teacher input. Support and feedback are given by all committee members.	An excellent opportunity for student to showcase work, student selects the persons who will guide and support learning, encourages collaboration and ongoing dialogue between student's support system.	Provide appropriate monitoring and scaffolding of social and academic development, create flexible schedules for conferences, maintain open and continual communication between members.

Dear Parents,

Our fall student-led conferences will be held at the end of October. Your child will be leading this conference. Your child will go through a portfolio of his or her work, the evaluation of his or her progress thus far this term, and share with you his or her goals for the remainder of the semester. The conference should last approximately 20 to 30 minutes. Please let me know what day and time is convenient for you to come, by marking the day and time on the form below. Please return this form to school by _____. I look forward to seeing you at the conference and hope that you will be able to participate.

Sincerely,

Student name _____

Please circle the day and time that is convenient for you.

Monday, _____   Tuesday, _____

5:00–5:30	4:00–4:30
5:30–6:00	4:30–5:00
6:00–6:30	5:00–5:30
6:30–7:00	5:30–6:00
7:00–7:30	6:00–6:30
7:30–8:00	6:30–7:00

After the parents return the letter of invitation stating what day would be most convenient for them to attend, and at least a week before the student-led conference, we recommend that the student write a letter to his or her parents personally inviting them to the conference. A sample letter written from a middle school student inviting his mother to come to the conference follows:

Dear Mom,

On Tuesday, _____, there will be a student-led conference for me. At the conference, we will look at my school progress, some of my work, and I will share with you my goals. It will take place in the classroom starting at _____. Thank you for your time, and I hope you will come.

Your son,

Time must also be given at the beginning of the year to explain and demonstrate to students what it means to respond to materials that have been selected for the portfolio. Brainstorming as a class or with a buddy can help the students think of the kind of work that should be placed in their portfolio. Then students can begin collecting and reflecting on the work samples that will be placed in their portfolio. These new pieces can be placed in the front of the portfolio.

Planning the Conference

The first step is to decide, as a class, on the conference format that will be followed. The next step is to discuss the order in which the items will be discussed. Some classes created an agenda to follow while others had students create an individual list, as long as they included everything identified on the class list. Examples of things that classes included on this agenda included portfolio, mathematics, writing journals, and "reading around the room," during which the student would show the parent the centers or work displayed.

Role-playing helps students prepare for conferences. This can be done with a buddy or a small group of four. If you choose to have the children practice in small groups, the children in the groups take turns portraying the teacher, parents, and student. The buddy system works well, too. The children share their work with a partner, then change roles. We were fortunate to be in an elementary building where students were practicing for their mid-year, student-led conferences. When practicing, they followed the list of activities that were selected as a class, including sharing portfolios, visiting room centers, sharing assignments, and sharing next term's goals.

It is also important that the class discuss goal setting. Some of the teachers we observed began this discussion by asking the students what areas they wanted to focus on during the next term. We have learned that many students create realistic and attainable goals. Many of the teachers we spoke to stated that they help their students identify what they want to achieve each term, semester, or year. The important thing to remember when assisting students with goal setting is to have them take responsibility for their own learning. In the classrooms we observed, we found that the students either created their own goals and then shared them with the teacher during a goal-setting conference prior to the conference or that the goals were established at the conference as the student and parent met with the teacher. Either way, when the goals are completed, they are placed into the portfolio.

During the Conference

During the conference, students need to have a clear sense of their role. The parent's and teacher's role is to support the child. Students may want to refer to the agenda or list of activities that were discussed in class that will guide them through the conference. An example of a check-off sheet that we observed students using in a lower elementary classroom contained the following: sharing portfolio (only the work that was selected for this term), goal sheet, "walk around the room" (visit one or two classroom centers), and assessments completed with the teacher. Assessments in this particular classroom consisted of the formal report card with a narrative portion, rubrics, and inventory sheets (e.g., reading, writing, and interest).

After the Conference

If portfolios are shared, it is important that the parents be informed that not all the materials will be discussed during the conference. In this case, some teachers have the parents take the portfolio home so that more time can be spent reviewing the contents. It is important to establish a date when the portfolio needs to be returned to school. We suggest having the child select one or two pieces and tell their parents why they selected them.

After the conference, the parents and the child should complete a feedback or reflection sheet. A sample form that the child could fill out might include the following questions:

- The part of the student-led conference that I enjoyed was: _____

- When I shared my work with my parents, I learned that I could: _____

- After leading the conference, I think I'll change _____ because _____

The students may also want to write a reflective entry in their journal or portfolio describing the conference, what went well, and what they would like to focus on during the next conference. The teacher and student could also debrief together, with the teacher writing notes and comments that could be considered when planning for the next conference.

It is also important to get feedback from the parents. This can be accomplished by asking the parent to write a letter to their child. This is an example of a letter that could be given to parents following a conference:

Dear Parents,

Please write a letter to your son or daughter reflecting on this conference. I have included some things you might want to focus on in this letter. This letter will be shared with your child at school and then placed in his or her portfolio. I would like to thank you again for participating in this conference and letting your child know that his or her education is important to you.

You may want to consider one or more of the following open-ended comments as you write your letter.

- What did you notice?
- What made you feel proud?
- I'd like to see you work on . . .
- Keep up the great work on/in . . .
- I know you sometimes have difficulty with _____, but I noticed that _____
- I am glad to see that you are . . .
- I am glad to see you are making an extra effort in . . .
- I think I could help with . . .
- I am glad to see you are working really hard in _____. You achieved a lot in pursuit of your goal.

Sincerely,

Reactions to Student-Led Conferences

When asked how they reacted to the student-led conference, feedback from parents, students, and teachers was overwhelmingly positive. Teachers and parents who were skeptical said that it was a pleasant surprise, and they now could not imagine conferencing any other way. Students said that they liked sharing their work with their parents. Teachers who have incorporated student-led conferences into their learning experiences felt sure that it is vital to the students' growth and development as learners.

Some teachers preferred holding a parent-teacher conference in November and a student-led conference in January. The rationale behind this was that portfolios are introduced and implemented during the first term; and the first conference, usually in November, typically lays the foundation for a working relationship between the parent and the teacher. By January, the teacher has had time to establish rapport with both students and parents; and students have become familiar with this type of assessment. Many of the teachers also shared that if a parent requests a parent-led conference in November, that request is accommodated.

Preparing for Parent-Teacher Conferences: Roles and Responsibilities

Student	Writes invitation for open-house/parent curriculum night, sets goals, selects work to be shared, writes reflection/reactions to work selected, writes invitation to parents and guardians.	Format 1: student not present; Format 2: student is listener and observer, Format 3: student proceeds with conference and shares work samples, journals, and center activities. Student engages parents in conversation and shares progress.	In formats 1 and 2, the student reviews the portfolio with parents at home. In format 3 the student reflects on the conference and completes evaluation form.
Teacher	Explains to parents the philosophy and procedures of classroom during open-house/parent curriculum night; assists in setting goals, collects work samples.	The teacher's role will depend on the conference format selected. In addition to the specified roles within each format, the teacher will facilitate the conference by providing appropriate support and encouragement.	Reflects on current instructional practices and finds alternative ways to scaffold learning and affirm goals.
Parent	Respond to child's invitation to both open-house/parent curriculum night and conference data; listens and asks question of teacher and/or student (depending on format); begins thinking about goals that could be considered.	Focus on child's work, listen and give appropriate feedback to either teacher and/or child (depending on format); ask probing questions for further detail during the conference; initiate conversation pertaining to concerns or issues about child's progress.	Suggest and add goals, complete feedback for classroom teacher and write letter to child.

In our conversations with parents and students of all grades regarding student-led conferences, the following reactions were given:

Cynthia: How do you feel about student-led conferences?

Parent #1:   I like the student-led conferences for several reasons: Your child doesn't think you're at school talking about them and wonder "What did my teacher say about me?"

The way they have it set up here is the kids write on the pages why they picked a certain thing so you know why they picked a certain thing and you sort of find out if your child really likes math—those are the pages she really likes or if she really likes writing or something [else].

A lot of times in a parent-teacher conference with the teacher, she'll hand you a portfolio and it will just be pages of math and you'll not have any idea and you'll look at it and it'll have numbers on it but when you look [at the pages] in a student-led conference, it says it is important to me because "it was hard at first and then I realized I figured it out and I did it."

It means something different than just looking at a page of math problems on it and that's why it's different. But I think if you feel you have a problem with your child that I think the parents feel that they can have a private conference with the teacher in addition to the student-led conference. I think that should be emphasized too. If you feel that your child's not quite fitting in or what ever problem they might have you have a second opportunity to have just a private conference with the teacher if there is a problem. I love student-led conferences.

Parent #2: I think it lets them show off their stuff that they're proud of and what they've done. I think if gives them confidence, and then it kind of shows the progress that they've made. I've already seen a lot of progress that he's done since the beginning first 9 weeks. So, I just think it kind of lets the parent know where they're at and stuff. What we need to work with at home.

Child #1: What I like about it is that I get to do the tour and show her papers that I did a long time ago and all of that. I choosed them because I thought my mom would like them and that what I did good at and I know I did good at, so I choosed them. I picked because they have patterns and all that with what they taught me.

Parent #3: The conferences are nice this way. It does give the child a chance to tell what they have learned and what they like about school. So it is productive.

Parent #4: My reaction is that he had to take the initiative to do it and that I thought it was good challenge. I'm sure that he'll look back and be glad he had the opportunity to do that. I was very proud of him for being able to pull it off.

Parent #5: I saw that he was taking ownership for his education because he is leading this conference. I think that is wonderful. I mean certainly the teacher is helping him along to do that,

Child #2:   but I mean he's taking ownership for his education and how well he does/doesn't do.

Child #2:   (The child does not respond but nods in agreement when his parents ask him several questions. He mentions that he agrees with what his parents said.)

Parent #6:   I think it makes the child feel really good about themselves to be able to share their work. So it's nice to see them in their environment, but away from other kids so they can spend some time to show you and talk with you and show you their progress. We've enjoyed them.

Child #3:   I get to lead them. [I] get to show what I wrote this school year.

Parent #7:   I think it's good that you have the kids involved in the conference because it gives them a good feeling about themselves. You have to realize that teachers can't do everything but parents have to be involved. So this way, the kids know you care about their work and that you're involved more than just helping at home, but you are interested in what they're doing in the classroom.

Comments and Concerns

What are some of the tricky situations that arise and how can they be avoided? Many potential problems can be avoided by clearly establishing the roles and responsibilities of the parent, student, and teacher during the student-led conference. Letters need to be sent home that will introduce and set the tone for the conference. If the parents are expecting a parent-teacher conference, they may go off in that direction and not follow their child's lead. Some teachers have met with the parents at the beginning of the year to introduce this method of conferencing and answer questions. The students need to understand their role and have ample time to prepare for the conference. The more information that all are given, the better able everyone will be to make the most of this opportunity to meet.

Reflections on Partnering

Teachers we interviewed became frustrated and discouraged with the traditional reporting process. Their reporting practices had to fit within a predetermined framework of percentages or grades established by the district or state, instead of being designed locally as a process of informing parents about their child's learning in ways that are meaningful for all stakeholders. For instance, Theresa, a fifth-grade teacher, commented, "What motivated me to make the change? I needed to find new ways to get my students to look at their work. I like change, and what's out there (e.g., report cards) isn't good so I was looking for alternatives." Brenda, a second-grade teacher we interviewed, shared the following thoughts regarding why she pursued other ways of informing parents: "I have shifted to a more process orientation enabling students to look more reflectively on student learning."

A primary goal of assessment, as we define it, is achieving a stronger link among instruction, assessment, and learning. Therefore, one should pursue learning and assessment in a manner that allows for the active engagement of students. The planning of activities and assessment of learning are things that can be done with students rather than to students. Within the traditional assessment paradigm, report card marks often reflect specific teaching strategies and styles adopted by the school district and tend to focus on an end product rather than a process. When teachers shift to a more negotiated, child-centered approach to assessment, the student is encouraged to take an active role in the learning process.

Student-led conferences are not merely activities—they are opportunities for the students to learn essential skills. The children learn how to look at their work, think about the direction they need to take for greater understanding, and set appropriate goals. They become the masters of their own learning. In addition to student sharing and learning, the teachers also can use student-led conferences as a time to pursue and reflect on their own instructional practices. For example, during her winter-term student-led conferences, Catherine, a fifth-grade teacher, realized that many of the parents were raising questions about the amount of time spent on mathematics homework and the frustrations they felt when trying to assist their child in completing these assignments. Hearing this, Catherine began to examine how she presented the mathematics concepts and decided to implement more inquiry-based, student-directed mathematics lessons. At the end of each mathematics session, students would work in small groups to discuss the assignment and to brainstorm and record possible strategies and solutions to complete these assignments. As a result of this shift in instructional practices, Catherine noticed an increase in parent-child communication and that both parents and students felt better about the assignments.

Additionally, she found that through the use of peer discussion, brainstorming, and recording possible strategies and solutions, the students were motivated and excited about formulating different ways to complete the homework. They also took on the role of teacher when sharing this information with their parents. Hence, this shift in instructional practices not only strengthened the parent-child relationship by encouraging the parent and child to review and discuss together the possible strategies and solutions for completing homework, but it also taught the students to work collaboratively in identifying and solving problems. What the students found most profitable was the time given to working with others while completing assignments.

The student-led conference can become an essential vehicle for teachers as they create and sustain a learning environment that promotes student autonomy. Within such an environment, roles and responsibilities shift to encourage students to make choices and to participate in the decision-making process about curriculum and learning. The teacher's role shifts to that of facilitator, mentor, and coach. The teacher provides stimulating activities that are age-appropriate and open-ended. Structured experiences provide a framework that encourages the child to be a producer rather than a consumer of knowledge. For instance, in one primary multi-age classroom, the children were given the opportunity to take responsibility for their learning by making choices from a list of activities that are negotiated by teacher and student that correspond to a particular theme. During our visit, the students were studying life cycles of chickens, caterpillars, and other bugs. Examples of "work choice" activities that students could select included journaling, recording observations in learning logs (including a picture of the observation with at least two sentences describing what was observed), silent reading or buddy reading, writing practice, mystery message, habitat mathematics, chick calendars, and endangered animal reports.

In another primary classroom, children's books—grouped by author, genre, or subject matter—were displayed throughout the room and within each curriculum center. Half the classroom housed the reading area and student publishing center. Charts, written reflections, and other student-created materials hung on the walls and on chart boards. Student learning logs were displayed near the science observatory on the south side of the room. One way students self-monitored and responded to learning was through a classroom computer program that recorded reading and writing progress. At this station, reading and writing scores were entered for each student as a way to maintain current levels of ability. The program noted learning progress that corresponded to the district's competency-based learning programs. In another elementary building, upper elementary students sat at round tables while completing reading and writing activities that evolved from author studies and class-generated themes. One entire wall was a mural that depicted the students' favorite storybook characters.

In each of these rooms, students made different choices that expanded on specific concepts that fit their needs. Each of these classrooms promoted a respectful and student-centered space in which the teacher and students worked together. The teachers in each of these classrooms assumed the role of a facilitator who guided, encouraged, and supported learning in a very individual way. Direct instruction was also available through strategy group lessons or in a whole group learning context. The students also took on multiple roles such as peer tutor, learner, and teacher.

Time and classroom space was used in a flexible manner to allow for in-depth questioning, exploration, and inquiry. Diversity and variation among students within each of these classrooms was anticipated, as they were encouraged to explore authentic learning experiences. As students assumed a more active role in their learning, ongoing reflection and self-evaluation was encouraged and valued. These students became authorities on their own learning.

A natural extension of this learning partnership is to link school-based learning to home environments. Parents become strong advocates for their child's learning and can also become valuable informants. With the parent, student, and teacher working collaboratively, they can become true partners in the learning process.

Ten

Assessment Troubleshooting

We should not assume that effective partnerships will be straightforward to implement. Parents and teachers may have difficulty unless they listen to each others concerns and are willing to learn from one another. teachers should establish communication as a core rather than secondary activity and plan on a range of activities for sharing, beginning to understand each others concerns, and building a working relationship. Sometimes, even with the best planning, tricky situations arise (see Bond, Tierney, Bertelsen, & Bresler, 1997). This chapter describes possible scenarios that could arise with parent-teacher and student-led conferences.

Student-Led Conferences

- What if the child freezes and forgets what to talk about?

Many teachers have a checklist so the children can make sure they know what to include in the conference. For example, younger children may follow picture clues as a way to conduct their conference. A note sent home immediately before the conference telling the parents exactly what the child will be focusing on is helpful. Parents can help the child stay focused, directing him or her back to the sheet if the child is unsure of what to do next. The checklist helps the child to stay on track. The teacher can also use the sheet for redirecting the student.

- What if the parents begin to talk to the teacher, leaving the student out of the conversation?

The best way to prevent this from happening is to set clear expectations prior to the conference. Make sure that the parents understand that their child will be directing the conference. If there are concerns that need to be addressed with the child and the teacher, respect the input from all. If the parents are only interested in the teacher's perspective, they need to be encouraged to schedule a separate conference. Let the parents know how they might schedule that conference (or better yet, schedule it right then and there) and let them know that you will be glad to discuss their concerns at that conference. In the meantime, you want the child to finish what he or she has prepared for this conference. Then redirect the conversation by asking the child about the next item on the agenda.

- What if the parents start correcting the child's work or sharing negative comments?

Again, this should be addressed in the letter to the parents. Remind the parents that they are going to see work samples at various stages. They are not to come to this situation with critical eyes. The purpose is to support the child and his or her learning. Their child and the teacher want to share more than the work; they are providing an opportunity for the parents to view the learning process. The end product does not always reflect this and should be regarded as a vehicle toward the child's thought processes. What lessons did she or he learn? What could she or he do better next time? How did the student feel about the work? The teacher can redirect the parents if they get off on a negative tangent by saying to the student, "What did you think about this project?" Often students are more critical of their work than anyone else in the room! They are aware of their strengths and weaknesses, and given the opportunity they will discuss them. The student can also redirect the parents if they start correcting work by saying that he or she realizes there are errors, and corrections will be addressed later. Be sure to help the student follow through with both correcting errors and letting parents know this was done.

- What if the parents start a conversation between themselves, leaving the child out?

With the full lives that parents lead today, it is easy for the parents to seize this opportunity to connect with each other. They may not have spoken to each other in weeks, and to be face to face is unusual and sometimes awkward. With the family structure changing, it is also possible to have two sets of parents present. This can be challenging because there are more interactions to direct. When a large group comes into the conference, the teacher needs to be ready to help the child manage the group. The goal of the conference is to focus on the child and his or her work. If there are two sets of parents, the teacher may want to schedule two conferences. This can be addressed in the initial communication to the parents. The parents and the child are set up for success when the roles and responsibilities are clearly defined. When parents get off track, the best thing to do is to redirect and refocus the conversation.

- What if students wish not to participate?

    It is important for students to take ownership of their learning and to feel confident in the learning process. The teacher needs to understand why the student may not want to participate. If it is a matter of "stage fright" then the teacher can provide opportunities for the students to practice with peers or the teacher prior to the conference. If the child is not wishing to participate because of feelings of inadequacy about his or her learning, it is important for the teacher to reassure the student and to assist him or her in preparing for the conference in a way that will enhance the positive aspects of learning. The teacher may also choose to schedule an individual conference at which the child and teacher will work together to write the goals and to select the materials to be shared.

    If there are difficulties at home which would preclude the child conferencing with his or her parents (e.g., an acute, stressful family problem), find an alternate adult such as a teacher, a minister, an adult relative, or a family friend whom the child knows and trusts so the child can have an opportunity to reflect on his or her work with a caring adult.

    With high school students there may be a feeling of discomfort with the mode of the conference and there is sometimes the issue of coordinating the conference with more than one teacher. We encourage you to consider alternative modes based upon your views of ways the partnership can be effectively negotiated. For example, some teachers have pursued an approach to conferencing in which they mediate between students and their families. They share the student's views of his or her goals and accomplishments and ask for the parents' views and suggestions. At some schools, parents are invited to attend student-led demonstrations or to view displays of work and goals as an opportunity to meet with the students and to talk with other parents. It may be preferable to establish ongoing mechanisms for parental engagements through periodic communications or events involving student exchanges.

Parent Reactions and Interactions

- What if the parents don't want to come to the conference?

    Teachers need to provide positive feedback and encouragement to both parents and students. The teacher can try alternative, nonthreatening approaches such as home visits, conference calls, letters home, and weekly journals. Conference calls and home visits are the most frequently used alternatives to a teacher conference.

    Sometimes parents need extra communication when it involves change. Many people resist change, especially when they do not understand the shift in expectations. Perhaps a phone call or a note of further explanation will help. By saying that this opportunity is something new and enlisting their feedback, parents may realize that their opinions are valued.

- What if one parent assumes the dominant role?

Prior to the conference, emphasize that the child would like both parents to participate in the discussion. Encourage the child to ask both parents what they think about a piece of work. The teacher can also help redirect the conversation by addressing each parent with a specific question or comment.

- What if other family members come to the conference?

In the letter sent home prior to the conference, remind parents that it would be preferable to leave siblings at home. It is important to ensure that the student has the full attention of his or her parents. At the same time, it is better to have the whole family there than no one at all if, for example, the parents do not have access to babysitting. Some teachers set up a play area for small children in the corner of the room. The school as a whole may take this opportunity to introduce younger siblings to the school they will be attending in a few years, providing childcare to the youngest, tours of the school for preschoolers, and appropriate activities for siblings who already attend the school.

- What if a parent comes in with a concern at an unscheduled time?

Validating the parent's concern is important. Tell the parent that you want to know his or her concerns, and you would like to set up a time when you can focus on those concerns. If at all possible, schedule the appointment while the parents are there. Explain that the children need you and the parent could not have your full attention at that time. You can also encourage them to write down their concerns so that each issue can be addressed at a more convenient time for both parent and teacher.

- What if the parents are unhappy with the quality of their child's work?

The teacher needs to be ready to discuss the child's present level of performance and to inform the parent if the child is working to his or her potential. If the teacher feels that the parents have unrealistic goals, then the teacher will need to report what the child can or cannot do through documentation such as observation, anecdotal accounts, and work samples. Displayed work samples provide an excellent benchmark to show what other children have produced. It may be helpful to discuss your plans for instruction for that child and the progress that you expect. Let them know what that progress may look like (e.g., your expectations that invented spellings will become more conventional and how you will support that in a student's development).

Teachers need to ask parents about the expectations they have for their child. It is important for the teacher to ask what the parents are unhappy about and to seek out ways that will be beneficial for all stakeholders (student, parent, and teacher). This is one area in which the teacher may wish to have the parents' input in drafting goals that will emphasize the expectations of both home and school.

- What if the parent has unrealistic expectations?

The teacher must be aware of the individual needs of students. In addition, the teacher must know what is going on in terms of social development and self-esteem and be able to recognize warning signs of students who are unable to handle pressure. It is important that the teacher and parents work together so that they can formulate realistic expectations and learning goals. The teacher, student, and parents could come to the conference with a list of strengths and areas of improvement which could serve as a springboard for goal setting.

- What if the parents start correcting the child's work or sharing negative comments?

Information about the curriculum and teacher expectations can be shared at a parent's night or curriculum night at the beginning of the year. It is important that the teacher continue to reinforce and share with parents that the conference will focus on student improvement and progress. It is important that both the teacher and parent praise the student for attempts and progress. It is also imperative that the teacher inform the parents at the outset of the conference that some of the work samples may be "works in progress."

- What if the conversation turns to grades and grading?

This is a very sensitive issue. At the beginning of the conference, the teacher may need to emphasize that this conference will focus on the student's progress and growth over the term rather than on specific grades. The student work samples will be especially useful when looking at a student's growth and learning over time. This strategy will focus the discussion on the student work samples rather than specific grades and scores.

- What if a parent does not agree with anything shared at the conference?

One of the goals of the conference is to establish a relationship between the teacher and the parents. In some cases this goal may take precedence over the goal of agreeing on the next steps a child might take in his or her education. The teacher might open the conference by asking the parents to share what has been successful for the child at home in previous years. In addition, you might present the student's portfolio and have the parents discuss their views of the student's progress.

As the parents speak, listen carefully without interrupting, and then paraphrase what they have told you to make sure that you understand their concerns. As you are listening, do not argue or try to construct arguments in your mind as they are speaking. Simply try to understand and communicate your understanding of their concerns—you can express your perspective later. Ask for clarification when you do not understand. Much resistance can be overcome just through listening and through letting others know that their messages are heard. However, this can only happen if you are willing to enter the world of the other through careful listening and to understand how his or her perspective is logical and sensible within that world.

See if you can find common ground. For example, both you and the parents are concerned about the education of this child. All of you want the best for this child. It is important for you to let the parents know that you share their concerns for high-quality education.

Consider what they are saying. Where is the source of the disagreement? Perhaps you have made a mistake or you have misunderstood something about that child. Best of all would be to apologize to the parents for the problem and then thank them sincerely for bringing it to your attention—as a means of laying groundwork for your relationship with them throughout the remainder of the year and later on with younger siblings. If you have made a mistake, the key is for you to avoid expressing anger, resentment, or the need to be right all the time.

Perhaps the parents have expectations about their children's education that you simply cannot meet. You can still let the parents know that you hear and understand their concerns through careful listening and reviewing their concerns with them. You can then let them know that you are limited in what you can do to accommodate their concerns. If there is something you can do that is reasonable within the framework of your classroom, then let them know what that might be. Do not, however, promise more than you can actually deliver.

Regular communication with parents is important for all students but critically so when there are disagreements between teacher and parents. Use class newsletters, personal letters, phone calls, and e-mail to let parents know the positive things that are happening in your classroom, particularly those that concern their child. Finally, let your administrator know about the nature of the difficulty and your response to it. As interactions continue to transpire, keep your administrator up to date on them.

Good Listening

Good listeners spend more time with their mouths shut and their ears open. While this sounds simple, it is not. Many times when we appear to be listening, we are actually composing a response—often in the form of an argument. Yet this kind of listening is counterproductive, particularly when one is trying to solve a problem or establish a relationship with a person with whom one has serious differences.

In order to be a good listener, one must take an active role. Good listening is not passive. Instead, good listeners take several positive actions. Here are some you can take.

- Reduce the other person's defensiveness by being sure you communicate openness. Avoid sitting across a desk from the other person. Ideally, you should sit in chairs that are facing at a 90-degree angle—facing straight across from each other increases defensiveness. A 90-degree angle allows you to communicate with less defensiveness.

- Consider also avoiding dressing in a way that communicates your superiority. Dress professionally and neatly but not many steps above than the parents with whom you will be working.

- Communicate respect. If the parent prefers using titles, then use them. Do not assume you are on a first-name basis until you have been invited to be so. This is particularly important in some communities (e.g., in many African-American families, children are taught to use titles and it is rude to assume that one can use an adult's first name without invitation).

- Your first goal is to understand how the person thinks—what is logical and sensible in this person's world? What are this person's goals and concerns? What is important to this person? You can find out these things not just from asking questions but through the stories he or she tells.

- Avoid the "third degree." One counseling strategy that may help is to avoid asking questions that begin with "why." A series of "why" questions can make a person feel defensive. As a teacher, you are already a person with authority, someone to be feared by people who have themselves had bad experiences with school. Instead of using "why," use the longer, wordy, passive voice (but effective) form: "how is it that." "How is it that Johnny comes to school without his homework?" is easier to answer than the same question with "why." This strategy also works with children.

- Communicate acceptance. Every person makes mistakes and does regrettable things. Some people's regrettable actions are more serious than others. However, we are all prone to making bad choices and mistakes. We can abhor a person's choices and still communicate respect for that individual as a human being. If you want to help people become more effective (e.g., helping parents to provide support for their children's intellectual growth), then communicating acceptance is an important first step. On the one hand,

cont.

it is very difficult for people to change when they feel negatively judged. On the other hand, when people are accepted for where they are, they can be helped (and they may welcome that help) to move forward.

- Watch and listen. Words may communicate one thing and body language another. Watch for both and for their congruence and contrasts. That may be important information for you to have.

- Tell the person that you want to understand and then check your understanding through paraphrasing what they say and asking if you have successfully understood them. After they have clarified their message or added to it, check again. You may need to spend a long time on this part of listening, yet that time is probably well spent.

- Avoid letting your own defensiveness come into play. That person may strongly disagree with what you have done. That is okay—we are all entitled to our opinions and that is what you are listening to, someone's opinion. It may or may not be truth; that is something else altogether to assess. As painful as it might be, if you can listen without defending and you can communicate that person's perspective back to him or her without mincing words about yourself, you will be well on your way to solving the problem instead of just arguing.

- You might feel very hurt about a situation. You may feel that you should be listened to first because of that hurt, that somehow it is unfair that you have to do all this listening and, in essence, give to someone who has done something you don't like. Find friends to talk with, where you can blow off steam before you go into a professional role that requires you to give in this manner. When you listen, you may come to a new understanding. A person's actions may make more sense to you and that may lessen the hurt.

- After the person has communicated his or her perspective, then there will be a time for you to communicate your perspective. When a person feels listened to, often they will be willing to listen back.

- There are situations that you will not be able to handle by yourself. If you feel this is the case, get support. Find a person who is a good listener, including a trained mediator if necessary, who can be a constructive part of the conversation.

- Finally, create a follow-through on the conversation. All your listening and relationship building will be for naught if you fail to follow through on agreements. People with whom you have difficulties do not trust you for one reason or another. The best way to build trust is by demonstrating trustworthiness through follow-up. Be sure to communicate about that follow-up. Do not, for example, make a referral and assume the referent will communicate with the parents. Your communication will keep new problems from building—you will become aware of the cracks that people can slip through and you will prevent that by being aware of what is going on.

Student Problems

- What if the student does not meet his/her goal?

We stress that the pursuit of goals is more important than some end achievement. Try to focus on the progress that was made—the successes and the learning that took place. The teacher should meet periodically with the student to review progress toward this goal, encouraging the student to document his or her growth through a visual such as a chart or timeline. This visual could include a timeline of individual tasks or the incremental steps that have been accomplished along the way. Attached to this visual and data log, the student could list specific outcomes and strategies to employ in the attainment of this goal. The visual and data log can then be shared with parents during the conference.

- What if the student is not motivated?

It is important that both the teacher and the parent ask the question, "What can I be doing to better respond to this student?" Teachers should keep expectations high for all students but should also take the time for individual interactions with students. During the conference with parents, it is important for the teacher to seek information from the parent on ways to develop and maintain motivation and an eagerness to learn. It is imperative that the child sees that the school and home are working together and that there is consistency in expectations between the school and home.

If attempts to reach out to the student fail to increase the child's motivation, it might appear that teachers and parents need to take complete charge of that student's learning. Yet the student still needs to be involved in the goal-setting portion of these conversations.

Where the problem is related to a lack of motivation, parents and teachers might have a private conference to discuss their concerns, review options, establish the basis for consistent expectations between school and home, and set up check points to ensure that progress is being made. They may want to consider whether the lack of motivation is a new problem or something ongoing. Perhaps there is a learning disability that has been undiagnosed. It may be necessary to look for concerns such as drug use or serious social problems (e.g., bullying or being an outcast) that may be impacting the student's schoolwork. If such problems exist, the first steps may be to address them before addressing learning.

The problem may be that the student does not have the maturity to create his or her own educational goals. If this is the case, then parents and the teacher need to offer the student some options. The student may not choose not to work, but he or she can make some choices about the subject matter of a large project. It would be a good idea to be as creative as possible about how a student's interests can be incorporated into the classroom. For example, how might a student investigate the history of video games and how might such a project help a student to learn critical literacy and other skills?

By giving the student some choice, parents and teachers are preparing the student to grow in the ability to make choices. The goal would be for the student to make more choices about his or her education in the next term, yet the student may remain behind his or her peers until he or she demonstrates the ability to make and follow through with goal-setting decisions. The student would be supported in this kind of growth through regular communication between teacher and parents, consistency in expectations between school and home, and interactions with more mature peers.

- What if the student has a learning or other kind of disability?

Well-established laws ensure appropriate education for students with disabilities.[1] An individualized approach to education for students with disabilities is congruent with what we are advocating—that a single classroom may accommodate many different educational goals and that every child should be working on educational goals that are appropriate and well-suited to him or her. The assessment artifacts described in previous chapters can certainly contribute to the conversation between parents, teachers, and disability experts.

What we would add to the procedures already established by law for children with disabilities is that the students themselves, as much as possible, become part of the process of establishing the individualized educational plan—setting the goals for learning. After all, the student him- or herself will have to deal with the disability for the rest of his or her life. Should not these children be given as much information as possible about how their minds and bodies work? Should not these children, in particular, have the opportunities to consider how they themselves learn and then be able to apply this information to new learning situations? All children need to have a voice in their own education; teachers and parents will find that there is a benefit to helping children develop goal setting and achievement strategies. Through these strategies, we are helping children develop skills that will help them reach their maximum potential.

Reflections on Educational Problem Solving

Assessment is a touchy process. Since it so often involves judgment, those who are being judged (and their parents) may well be suspicious of the people who are doing the judging. Assessment is a mirror, at best it is welcomed because its reflection is known to be a true and accurate source of knowledge about oneself. Better to look in the mirror and fix the problems that gaze back before those problems become visible to people in the world at large. At worst, assessment is a not-so-fun-house mirror, distorting its subject in unflattering ways, and worse than useless because of the ways in which assessment processes open and close gates in our society.

The stakes are high and getting higher as more and more governmental bodies demand certain kinds of assessment processes and attach stakes such as the possibility of graduation for students or the possibility of raises in salary for teachers to the results. Where there are conflicts and problems in assessment, it is important to retain a sense of empathy for all the stakeholders—understanding the pressures administrators are under in terms of their district's demands, understanding students who know they must take certain kinds of tests but would much rather not, understanding parents who have had negative experiences themselves with assessment and do not want their children to go through the same pain, understanding parents whose self-esteem may be connected with how well their children do, understanding fellow-teachers who are struggling to complete state-mandated assessments and who cannot conceive of adding yet one more task to their busy schedules. We may not agree, but we can nevertheless understand. That understanding, coupled with compassion and respect, can create the groundwork for a workable partnership among people who differ in philosophy and stance.

Endnote

1   In accordance with the United States Individuals with Disabilities Education Act and the Code of Federal Regulations, parents must participate

- in discussions regarding the information that will be incorporated into the evaluation process, which may also include the parents providing additional information about the child (§300.533 (a) (1) (i)

- as a member of the team that determines eligibility (§ 300.534 (a) (1))

- as a member of the team who makes placement decisions (§ 300.501 [c])

- in the development of their child's IEP as it relates to the child's participation in the general curriculum (§ 300.347 (a) (5) (i) (ii) (A) (B))

Hence, the IDEA statute and the Federal Regulations indicate that parents of children with disabilities are expected to be equal participants in the education of their children. This means that decisions regarding the educational services afforded their child must be made in concert with other school or agency personnel. Examples of information that a parent may provide during a conference (or IEP meeting) include the following:

- critical information regarding the strengths of their child and expressions of their concerns for enhancing the education of their child
- input about the child's need for special education and related services and supplementary aids and services
- the degree to which their child will be involved and progress in the general curriculum and participate in state and district-wide assessments
- what services the agency will provide to the child in what setting. (34 C.F.R. Part 300. Appendix A, p. 104)

In addition, several regulations speaks specifically to the rights of parents of children with special needs:

- Access to inspect and review any education records relating to their child (§ 300.562 (a) (b) (1) (2) (3) (c).
- Written consent before the school district can disclose any information about a child with disabilities (§ 300. 571(a) (1)).
- Informed parental consent before conducting an initial evaluation or reevaluation (§ 300.505 (a) (i) (ii) (2) (3) (i) (ii)).
- Notification to participate in meetings regarding the education of their child (§ 300.501 (a) (1) (i) (ii) (2) (i) (ii) (b)). School districts must ensure that the parents will participate in these meetings. Notification of such meetings may include individual or conference telephone calls and/or video conferencing (§ 300.501 (4)).

Parental participation involves the following:

- Notifying the parents of the meeting with ample time to ensure their attendance (§ 300.345 (a) (1).
- Documenting the number and type of correspondence to ensure parental participation (§ 300.345 (2) (i) (ii) (3) (c)).

Part IV

Reflections on the Assessment Journey

Eleven

A Conversation About Issues

- What are the goals of the book?

Rob: We hope that the book will spur inquiry and reflection on the challenge of creating assessment practices that support more meaningful partnerships. We are keen to pursue a form of assessment that involves different partnerships than our past assessment practices. Our goal is to develop a partnership with the student, caregivers, teachers, and others that creates a synergy and support system for learning as all parties work together rather than against or apart from one another. Although this may sound simple, we have found it is not. We see the development of meaningful partnerships as complex and demanding. Our suggestions and deliberations illustrate some of the possibilities as well as some factors and issues to consider.

Tom: One of the threads of this book is that a partnership among students, teachers, and parents is critical to developing a culture of meaningful assessment in classrooms and schools. If we reconceptualize assessment in this way, the spirit of how we go about developing and implementing assessment practices shifts from an overly focused agenda of ranking, comparing, and categorizing to one of mutual support and progressive refinement. In a partnership relationship there is space for diverse views, spirited discussion, and multiple paths toward achieving goals with the overarching understanding that assessments being developed promote learning rather than constrain it. If assessment is viewed in this way, it does not diminish the seriousness of the task, the rigor of the work, or the desire for fair, just evaluation. Rather, it increases these features. To cultivate this spirit of partnership, we present some ways of thinking about, implementing, and reporting assessments that involve ongoing negotiations, collaborative decision making, and rich descriptions of what learners are doing.

Cynthia: I see this book as a resource for administrators, teachers, and parents that will provide support for them in their journey toward developing more learner-based assessment practices that capture student interest, strengths, and learning modalities. It is my hope that administrators and teachers will find this book useful as they begin to develop partnerships with parents and students. The ideas shared in this book can also encourage parents to become more involved in the decision-making process regarding their child's learning. Through the links among the different assessment strategies described throughout the book, it is my hope that all stakeholders can implement new ideas within their educational programs, while encouraging ongoing dialogues about teaching and learning.

Ernie: Learning is ongoing, embedded in social relationships, and situated in a contextual space. Each student has particular learning styles and perspectives but each student also belongs to interpretative communities, including the cultures of the classroom, the home, and peer groups. Constructivist theories of learning, learner-centered education, and culturally responsive instruction all stress being sensitive to the learning patterns and the goals of the students (Delpit, 1995; Ladson-Billings, 1994). The emphasis on student knowledge shifts from molding the learners to fit the material to more of a transactional model wherein materials are chosen for the classroom in response to students' needs, desires, and ways of knowing. In such a model teachers can capitalize on student strengths.

Contextualizing instruction will not be as effective without allowing assessments to meet local needs and the complexities of the classroom. Assessments need to be tailored to the individual, to the classroom, to the school, and to the community. Assessments developed with the learner and taking into account the needs and expectations of the parents and the community are more in line with constructivist learning. Also, the teacher must learn about students in order to respond to their needs and help evaluate their progress. Contextualized assessment, therefore, becomes essential to the teacher's culturally responsive approaches in the classroom.

- What are the origins of the notion of "assessment partnerships and interactive assessment"?

Rob: The concept of assessment partnerships and notion of interactive assessment began several years ago when Tom and I were interested in extending learner-centered assessment to address the issue of report cards. We were concerned with the content of most report cards and the relationship among teachers, students, and learning that they mirrored. The narrow set of descriptors and grading practices seemed a far cry from the richness of a portfolio or from descriptive conversations around student work. While learner-centered assessment focuses upon the students and stakeholders assuming responsibility for assessing themselves in partnership with teachers, report cards are done by the teacher with little input from others.

A mystery emerged as we looked at the history of report cards. We were intrigued to uncover a history of attempts to reform report card practices dating back at least 100 years. Furthermore, some of the examples of innovative report cards were as interesting as the variations developed by districts looking for change today. Why was it that these innovations were never able to be sustained? Perhaps report cards serve a kind of ritualistic function which parents and students have come to expect. Perhaps report cards have not changed because most innovations focused on content or form but not on function. The function has always been to inform parents and students of the teacher's assessment, rather than to engage parents, students, and teachers in joint decision making.

In pursuit of answers to these and other questions, we spent the next several years studying assessment reforms, especially reforms that involved report cards or parent-teacher-student partnerships. Cynthia and Ernie joined us as we began the first of several studies. We began a weekly get-together at which we discussed these matters and our observations. Often, we behaved as if we were investigative reporters as we pursued "leads" and searched for teachers who were exploring alternatives. Sometimes we had the good fortune of having friends and colleagues who became interested in what we were doing and pursued these notions in their classrooms. This book represents the fruits of our observations, analyses, and discussions.

The book's focus shifted from practices that might be viewed as alternatives or supplements to report cards to a notion of assessment relationships as the cornerstone of any thinking about assessment practices including portfolios, conferencing, and report cards. All of us involved in the project, including Tom, Rob, Ernie, Cynthia, Jane Bresler, Carolyn Cutler, and the teachers who became our partners realized that the relationship among teachers, students, and parents was key.

• Can you define assessment partnerships and interactive assessment?

Tom: Assessment partnerships and interactive assessment on concepts we are using to push our thinking about assessment in some new ways. Primarily the notions of interactive assessment and assessment partnerships involves recognizing that ongoing relationships are central to assessment; relationships among students, teachers, parents, and others are key to the growth and achievement of the learner. The purpose of these relationships is to negotiate a variety of assessment practices that honor the multifaceted nature of learning, help set goals that continue to inform growth, re-inform teaching, and create communities of learners who support and value one another. In a sense we are proposing a shift towards a different type of validity, what we call transactional validity. With this concept, we emphasize that to be valid, or to assess what it purports to assess, assessments have to consider the give-and-take among stakeholders who develop assessments within shared understandings. For example, students, teachers, and others might develop an assessment relationship that facilitates the collection of authentic samples of the student's progress, a way to reflect upon the how and why of that collection process, media to represent the samples and the process in a systematic way, and the means to engage the stakeholders in decision making and goal setting. The validity of such assessments rests upon how effectively the stakeholders negotiate assessment practices that draw upon shared communal guidelines while allowing for individual creativity. Acknowledgment of reciprocal interactions between the individual and the guidelines becomes an important feature of the assessment relationship and are central to interactive assessment.

If we reconceptualize assessment in this way, the spirit of how we go about developing and implementing assessment practices shifts from an overly focused agenda of ranking, comparing, and categorizing to one of mutual support and progressive refinement. In a healthy relationship there is space for diverse views, spirited discussion, and multiple paths towards achieving goals with the overarching understanding that the assessments being developed promote learning rather than constrain it. If assessment is viewed in this way, it does not diminish the seriousness of the task, the rigor of the work, or the desire for fair, just evaluation. Rather, it increases these features. To cultivate this spirit of partnership, we present some ways of thinking about, implementing, and reporting assessments that involve ongoing negotiations, collaborative decision making, and rich descriptions of what learners are doing.

Rob: We are working to develop a form of assessment that involves better and different partnerships than our past practices tended to perpetuate. Traditionally, grades and report cards have been prepared by teachers for parents, students, and others. We are interested in ways that we might develop assessment and reporting practices that provide for the meaningful participation of students and their parents. While we understand why teachers and others rely on traditional practices, we do not think that their reasons are adequate. Traditional methods of reporting to parents perpetuate a disengagement of students and parents from ongoing and meaningful negotiation around learning. Our goal is to develop a partnership with the student, caregivers, teachers, and others that creates a synergy and support system for learning as all parties work together rather than against or apart from one another. Essentially, we are suggesting a new ethic for testing that is anchored in notions of relationships.

- Could you talk more about transactional validity?

    Rob: As we talked about validity, I was contemplating how others have been interested in expanding the concept of validity to be more inclusive. I was reminded of the concept of responsive evaluation that Robert Stake (1983) proposed and how we were actually pushing beyond it to include a multiple perspective responsiveness that focused on transactional relationships in assessment. For us transactional implies that there is an exchange/transaction/negotiation rather than merely procedural interaction. To capture these ideas we are labeling them transactional validity.

Cynthia: In our past experiences in classrooms, teachers have attempted to change portions or parts of their assessment practices without recognizing that they were shifting the teaching and learning as well. In this sense, transactional validity is about seeing assessment as a series of transactions that are informing practices like student-led conferences, portfolios, and other assessments on multiple levels simultaneously.

Ernie: Transactional validity reconnects assessment to learning by reconceptualizing and reimagining possibilities for assessment relationships. These relationships are negotiated as stakeholders recognize that setting learning goals involves understanding the complex transactions involved in representing individual development.

- Tell me more about your dissatisfaction with traditional assessment practices.

Tom: Our goals are to support inquiry, not prescribe answers, to build relationships, not disengagements, with students and their parents, to honor the expertise of all stakeholders, not diminish voices, and to continually question how assessment practices are linked to teaching and learning. In working toward these goals, we present and explore assessments that are field-tested in a variety of classrooms. Our own research suggested to us that traditional testing and report cards may present a diminished or even reductionist picture of a learner's growth and achievements. In our view, portfolios, student-led conferences, new technologies such as websites, exhibitions, and other assessments provide a richer, more learner-centered portrait of learning. However, we recognize that merely replacing one form of assessment with another is not adequate or necessarily empowering. Along with this replacement, we see a need for reconceptualizing the relationships associated with assessment. What we are trying to accomplish in this book is the reconceptualization of partnerships in which assessment is informed by a spirit of advocacy for students.

- So how would you hope to see teachers or schools move ahead in terms of the notion of assessment partnerships and interactive assessment?

Rob: It is important to come to grips with the goals and principles that underpin your learning community. I would encourage an emphasis upon respect as well as joint decision making. Then as the various classes begin to explore these notions, they need to have opportunities to share insights, discuss concerns, and set goals. I would discourage a one-size-fits-all standard for practice.

Tom: I see schools as nested learning communities. In a community practice context, I think partnerships need to be negotiated and renegotiated as a central feature of crafting an assessment framework with the understanding that each school site would implement, revisit, and refine these as part of learning and teaching.

• So how about these notions in the context of larger school change?

Cynthia: I agree with Tom's thoughts on negotiating and renegotiating. Research on school reform indicates that schools implement either incremental or fundamental, tend to change systemic efforts (Cuban, 1993). Incremental or piece meal reform efforts, to my mind, just tinker with one or more aspects of the educational system. Some may view these efforts as "add-ons" that typically respond to a current issue, usually one that is voiced from an outside source, as a way to fix the problem. Systemic reform, on the other hand, is a restructuring of the entire educational system to address concerns or problems. It is my belief that if a reform initiative does not address the entire educational system, then one is advocating for incremental rather than systemic change. I agree with Cuban and others who support systemic educational reform, in that I believe all aspects of the educational system need to be addressed. The piecemeal or incremental approach to school reform has historically not been successful. Change takes time, thought, strategic planning, and ongoing dialogue among stakeholders. Some fail to see that an in-depth look at the broader picture through a long-range planning program is paramount when contemplating educational reform. Such planning needs to include integrating what we are discussing into curriculum development and assessment, scheduling, classroom environment, teacher professionalism and development, and student learning and expectations.

Ernie: One thing that we have noted again and again in our work with teachers involved in new assessment practices is that they often feel isolated in their efforts. These individuals, small groups, and occasionally the entire faculty of a school endure the hard work of developing a means of assessment that they feel will improve their students' education. However, they tend to do so on their own. This has several repercussions: teachers end up reinventing the wheel, they do not benefit from a strong support system, and their efforts either remain isolated in one classroom or die out altogether.

• But aren't schools moving in other directions, especially those schools that place so much emphasis upon traditional forms of testing or standardized tests?

Rob: That may be all the more reason that such a relationship is important. Teachers, students, and parents need to be working together so that they can be informed but not overrun by results from tests such as these. In those states where tests are used for high-stakes decisions, conversations between teachers, parents, and schools should subsume such results and not be subsumed by them. In other words, any decisions need to emanate from the discussions between teachers, parents, and students and not just from test results.

Of course, we are disturbed that high-stakes testing is being used to make important decisions regarding students' futures, including closing doors. Sometimes students are retained based upon such tests or are not allowed to graduate. We see this as problematic on a number of fronts.

Ernie: One of the striking inconsistencies in our system of education is that while more and more educators have advocated approaches to learning that address the diverse needs of students, various cultural ways of knowing, and family and community expectations and involvement, schools nationwide have felt pressure to prove their merit by subjecting their students to high-stakes testing. Standardized proficiency tests are now being used to determine whether students move on to the next grade, whether schools get funded, whether principals retain their jobs. Teachers in various grade levels currently spend a large portion of their classroom time preparing students for such tests. Rather than reading books or conducting scientific experiments, these students practice taking tests. Ironically, studies have shown that even when a school raises its scores on a particular standard exam, scores will drop immediately if the district switches to a different test. The knowledge learned is not transferable to other testing situations, much less to real life.

In discussing assessment practices, however, standardized testing cannot be disregarded. As long as politicians and administrators are looking for a quick fix, teachers will have to find ways to integrate these tests into their classrooms without totally disrupting the learning environment.

Rob: If legislatures force us to conduct high-stakes assessment then I think it should be done as thoughtfully and with as much planning as possible. This entails a fuller consideration of student performance beyond standardized tests or proficiency tests, a consideration that involves a decision-making partnership with students, parents, and other sponsors.

Cynthia: Linda Darling-Hammond (1993) suggested that there are two very different notions of school reform sometimes working in parallel, but mostly working at cross-purposes. One focuses on "tightening the controls—more tests, more directive curricula, more standards enforced by more rewards and more sanctions" (p. 754). The other focuses more on developing schools that are inquiring and collaborative learning communities.

- Can you say more about teachers reinventing the wheel and the sustainability of these efforts?

Ernie: Teachers who try to utilize narratives, conferences, or portfolios may have learned these methods in school, from conferences or workshops, or from professional journals. They may even have developed a method all their own. Many do wonderful, exciting things with these forms of assessment in their classrooms. Yet we were surprised to learn that district teachers who are involved in similar innovative practices rarely traded tips, discussed concerns, or networked.

Other teachers who are interested in developing new means of assessment seldom have opportunities to meet with and learn from teachers who are already engaged in these practices. So each teacher or group of teachers develops portfolio assessment from scratch, taking information from books, journals, or workshops, but not benefiting from the efforts of other teachers who may have had similar experiences, similar glorious moments, and similar problems.

Often, teachers working in isolation have no one to turn to when things go wrong, no one to share a moment with over the small successes. When a parent complains or a plan fails, there is no one saying, "Yeah, that happened to me, but then . . . " Without feedback from other teachers, even minor problems may seem like failures. Each time a new situation is encountered the teacher has to revise his or her practices without the benefit of knowing what other teachers have done in similar contexts. Their efforts may remain in one site or die out because their changes are not systemic. If a single teacher in a school is using portfolios, students enter the class unused to the system and parents expect the grades their child received in other years; and even if the administration thinks that what the teacher is doing is interesting, it is not likely to go out of its way to be supportive. Many teachers give up and capitulate to the system.

Conferences, retreats, meetings, and best practices seminars are one way to spread ideas around. These events introduce teachers to assessment practices, but they tend to be infrequent. It could prove to be much more beneficial to have a newsletter in which teachers could share their own ideas—or, even better, a website that could offer both suggestions and dialogue concerning assessment practices.

As they move ahead, teachers need to inform others. Grades and proficiency tests still receive more attention from the media, however. Although alternative assessments have been around for years a majority of community members will be more familiar with traditional assessment tools. In conjunction with partnering with parents, it is essential for teachers to educate parents, administrators, community, and other teachers about what they are doing and why.

Cynthia: As we continue to explore the roles of teachers, students, and parents through the lens of the community of learners, it becomes evident that all the stakeholders must be active participants in negotiating goals and in deciding how the goals will be achieved. Emphasis is placed on the learning process rather than the outcome, and the communication efforts between and among all parties are enhanced. Through this collaborative effort, both parents and teachers can enhance student learning and assist students in making the necessary connections.

One reccurring theme that we noted in our initial research into local assessment reform initiatives was the need for learning communities—parents, teachers, students—that work together as they develop "a new web of relationships through the school" (Lieberman & Miller, 1990, p. 763). These relationships emphasize learning that provides insights into a "new system that must no longer hold time constant and allow achievement to vary . . . there is no other way to accommodate the facts that different children learn at different rates and have different learning needs" (Reigeluth, 1994, p. 7).

- Are there any legal issues related to parental involvement in assessment?

Rob: I think that any form of assessment needs to be reviewed for its congruence with laws and ethics. I believe that the approach to assessment that we are suggesting has merit and may be a more judicious way to make decisions about students' lives and their futures. I suspect that assessment partnerships could ensure that all of the interested parties have a voice in decision making that is consistent with what we deem important ethical principles. But before these steps could replace other practices (e.g., state or provincially mandated testing), it would be advisable to review state and provincial laws that might apply. In some countries, specific tenets would need to be followed, especially in terms of the procedures that might be necessary for the practice to pass muster in the courts.

- Advance notice needs to be provided to parents and others of their intentions to use classroom-derived performance measures.
- Procedures need to be reviewed by constituencies.
- There needs to be a relationship to learning objectives.
- Acceptable performance-based measures need to be included.
- Practices need to be examined for bias, such as language or cultural bias.
- Consensus on evaluative criteria needs be pursued.
- Procedures for dual evaluation need to be developed.
- Adequate sampling of performance should be provided.

Cynthia: I also think that it is important that parents and teachers recognize that legally they need to pursue a partnership similar to what we are proposing. This partnership includes parents and teachers of both general and special education students. In those situations involving students with special needs, the standards set forth by legal guidelines require the school to seek input by the parents into what can be done to improve the student's performance. Indeed, I believe that the guidelines for special needs students might serve as a basis for thinking through these principles.

- Any last words?

Tom: It has taken us a long time to get to where we are now: lots of visits to schools and classrooms, time studying and restudying great teachers, and an ongoing discussion of issues over several years. I would suggest that they share some essential characteristics. Primarily, classrooms should be invitational spaces where students, parents, caregivers, and others can engage in assessment conversations with teachers if necessary. Assessment options are developed as a feature of relationships or partnerships among students, teachers, parents, caregivers, and other stakeholders. It may not be necessary for all partners to be equally engaged all the time in these choices. For example, it does seem practical for parents to be a part of every decision made in a classroom context concerning assessment. The student and the teacher may take a stronger lead in this area. However, parents and other stakeholders should be regularly apprised of the purpose of assessments and what assessments are indicating about student progress. In so doing, as we have suggested throughout the book, part of the challenge of educative assessment is the necessity to advocate with student, parents, and administrators that no single assessment can fully capture student learning achievement. Assessment is intricately bound up with learning. Even if learners and teachers are feeling pressure to focus on standardized assessments because of district and state mandates or desires for getting into college, to exclude assessments like portfolios, presentations, exhibitions, and other learner-directed assessments creates a false hierarchy. I think that we develop assessment options within a coherent framework so that stakeholders are not overwhelmed by assessment tasks. This framework needs to be crafted collaboratively by stakeholders including students, parents, caregivers, building-level and district-level administrators. It should be elastic enough so that schools can tailor it to individual needs. The framework must include an assessment philosophy, purposes, and specific goals for assessment, as well as legal considerations, stakeholder rights, and processes for appeal and negotiation. Recommendations for specific practices may be included, but these should be refined at the school level so that local knowledge and expertise is honored. Finally, I think record keeping is important, especially within the context of using different assessment options.

Cynthia: I think this book represents what the third wave or cycle of reform hopes to achieve. We hope teachers are willing and able to take an active role in advocating for and designing assessment practices that are not only aligned with their teaching philosophies and practices, but will also invite and encourage ongoing conversations with parents and students. The suggestions that we have offered provide possibilities that teachers, students, and parents could pursue in their quest for more interactive assessment practices. These possibilities shift the decision-making process from external forces to individual teachers, students, and parents. We hope this book will encourage teachers to create and nurture partnerships with their students and parents.

We believe that for systemic reform efforts to be sustained, initiatives should begin in the classroom with the teachers leading the initiative. By taking this stance, we have designed this book to assist teachers in their journey toward more student-directed assessment practices. We hope that these assessment possibilities are not used as just an add-on but as a way of developing better relationships, including viable ways to gather documentation of both teaching and learning.

I believe learner-based assessment can be useful. It is important that teachers as well as parents begin to see the world through a student's eyes in order to understand what is being tested and what is truly relevant, meaningful, and useful to children as they continue to grow and learn. Moreover, students need to learn how to learn including responsible decision making.

I would like to see teachers use this book as a resource to build upon what they already know about teacher and learning. This book could extend teachers' assessment practices by illustrating how they can incorporate more learner-based assessments into their teaching and learning in addition to what is required. When exploring the roles of teachers, students, and parents through the lens of learner-based assessment relationships, it becomes evident that the teacher, student, and parent become active participants who negotiate the goals and decide how these goals can best be achieved. Emphasis is placed on the learning process rather than just the outcome. This issue also influences the school culture through curriculum study and development, climate setting, and social interactions between student and teacher, student and parent, and teacher and parent. The influence that learner-based assessment practices have on parents and the community can only enhance the communication efforts. Through this collaborative effort, both parents and teachers can assist students in making the necessary connections between school, functional, work place, and home literacy.

Where to From Here?

There is an old aphorism about traveling and taking journeys that states that the map is not the terrain. This could be interpreted to mean that the actual trip is different from any map we set out to follow. In one sense this book creates a new map for assessment changes. As we attempt to follow our own map through teaching courses, institutional reviews, and work with schools and individual teachers, the terrain will be different. Furthermore, the assessments we have described in this book will play out differently in various schools and classrooms as stakeholders develop partnerships or relationships as foundations to their assessment practices. We believe this will be a positive outcome. Our goal from the beginning has been to open possibilities for assessment, not to constrain them, to build on local expertise, not to undermine it, to encourage ways to make assessment visible, not to cloak it, and to intimately link assessment with teaching and learning for all stakeholders. We hope to continue our own journeys.

References

Allington, R., Butler, A., & Tierney, R. (1993). Teachers' guide to evaluation. Glenview, IL: Scott Foresman.

Barrs, M., Ellis, S., Hester, H., & Thomas, A. (1988). *The primary language record.* Portsmouth, NH: Heinemann.

Beeth, M. E., Cross, L., Pearl, K., Pirro, J., Yagnesak, K., & Kennedy, J. (2001, March 4). A continuum for assessing science process knowledge in grades K–6. *Electronic Journal of Science Education.* [On-line serial]. Available: http://unr.edu/homepage/crowther/ejse/beethetal.html.

Bertelsen, C., & Bresler, J. (1997) Conferencing with students and parents. Unpublished materials.

Bertelsen, C., Tierney, R. J., Crumpler, T., Bond, E., & Bresler, J. (1997). *Aligning report cards with assessment reform in literacy: Studies of shifting philosophy and practice.* National Reading Conference, Phoenix, AZ.

Black, P., & William, D. (1998). Assessment and classroom learning. *Assessment in Education, 5* (1), 7–75.

Bond, E., Tierney, R. J., Bertelsen, C.B., & Bresler, J. (1998). *A confluence of agendas and power relationships: Student-led conferences.* Phoenix, AZ: National Reading Conference.

Bruner, J. (1990). *Acts of meaning.* Cambridge, MA: Harvard University Press.

Carini, P. F. (1994). Dear Sister Bess—An essay on standards, judgement, and writing. *Assessing Writing, 1* (1), 29–65.

Carter, M. (1992). Self-assessment using writing portfolios. Unpublished doctoral dissertation, Ohio State University, Columbus.

Clark, C. T., Chow-Hoy, T., Herter, R. J., Moss, P. A., & Young, S. (1996, April). *Beyond product: Portfolios, motivation, and engagement.* Paper presented at the annual meeting of the American Educational Research Association, New York.

Crumpler, T. (1996) *Exploring a culture of assessment with ninth grade students: Convergences of meaning within dramas of assessment.* Unpublished doctoral dissertation, Ohio State University, Columbus.

Cuban, L. (1993). *How teachers taught: Constancy and change in American classrooms 1880-1990* (2nd ed.). New York: Teachers College Press.

Darling-Hammond, L., Ancess, J., & Falk, B. (1995). *Authentic assessment in action studies of schools and students at work.* (Series on School Reform). New York: Teachers College Press.

Davies, A. (2000). *Making classroom assessment work.* Merville, British Columbia: Connections.

Delpit, L. (1995). *Other people's children: Cultural conflict in the classroom.* New York: Norton.

Fenner, L. (1995). *Student portfolios: A view from inside the classroom.* Unpublished doctoral dissertation, Ohio State University, Columbus.

Guba, E. G., & Lincoln, Y. S. (1989). *Fourth generation evaluation.* Newbury Park, CA: Sage.

Hoffman, J. V., Assaf, L. C., & Paris, S. G. (2001). High stakes testing in reading: Today in Texas, tomorrow? *The Reading Teacher, 54* (5), 482–488.

Johnston, P. H. (1993). Assessment as social practice. In D. J. Leu & C. K. Kinzer (Eds.), *Examining central issues in literacy research, theory and practice* (pp. 11–24). Chicago, IL: National Reading Conference.

Kohn, A. (1993). *Punished by rewards: The trouble with gold stars, incentive plans, A's, praise and other bribes.* New York: Houghton Mifflin.

Ladson-Billings, G. (1994). *The dreamkeepers: Successful teachers of African American children.* San Francisco: Jossey-Bass.

Lather, P. (1986). Research as praxis. *Harvard Educational Review, 56* (3), 257–277.

Lieberman, A., & Miller, L. (June 1990). Restructuring schools: What matters and what works. *Phi Delta Kappan, 71* (10), 759–764.

Madaus G. F. (1988). The influence of testing on the curriculum. In L. N. Tanner (Ed.), *Critical issues in curriculum* (pp. 83–121). Chicago, IL: University of Chicago Press.

Moss, P. A. (in press). The meaning and consequences of reliability. *Journal of Educational and Behavioral Statistics.*

Moss, P. A. (1996). Enlarging the dialogue in educational measurement: Voices from interpretive research traditions. *Educational Researcher,* 25 (1), 20–28, 43.

Moss, P. A., & Shutz, A. (2001). Educational standards, assessment, and the search for consensus. *American Educational Research Journal, 38* (1), 37–70.

Reigeluth, C. M. (1994). Introduction: The imperative for systemic change. In C. M.

Reigeluth, F. M., & Garfinkle, R. J. (year). *Systemic change in education.* Englewood Cliffs, NJ: Educational Technology.

Serafini, F. (2001). Three paradigms of assessment: Measurement, procedure and inquiry. *The Reading Teacher, 54* (4), 384–393.

Shavelson, R., Baxter, G. P., & Pine, J. (1992). Performance assessment: Political rhetoric and measurement reality. *Educational Researcher, 21* (4), 22–27.

Short, K., Harste, J., & Burke, C. (1995). *Creating classrooms for authors and inquirers.* Portsmouth, NH: Heinemann.

Stake, R. (1983). The case study method in social inquiry. In G. Madaus, M. Scriven, & D. Stufflebeam (Eds.), *Evaluation models* (pp. 279–286). Boston: Kluwer-Nijhoff.

Stiggins, R. (1997). *Student-centered classroom assessment* (2nd ed). Columbus: Merrill.

Tierney, R. J. (1998). Negotiating learner-based literacy assessments: Some guiding principles. *The Reading Teacher 51* (5), 374–391.

Tierney, R. J., Carter, M., & Desai, L. (1991). *Portfolio assessment in the reading-writing classroom.* Norwood, MA: Christopher-Gordon.

Tierney, R. J., Clark, C. (with Fenner, L., Herter, R. J., Staunton Simpson, C., & Wiser, B.) (1998). Portfolios: Assumptions, tensions, and possibilities. *Reading Research Quarterly*, 33 (4), 474–486.

Tierney, R. J., Crumpler, T., Bond, E., Bertelsen, C., & Bresler, J. (1998). *Reforming assessment practices: Negotiating spaces for agency via report cards and conferences.* Austin, TX: National Reading Conference.

Index

Achievement, 26, 32
Assessment,
    challenges in shifting, 12–13
    collaborative; *see* Community;
      Inquiry, collaborative;
      Partnership
    digital, 29, 101–117
    examples of, 61–64
    learner-centered, 12, 13
    as a means, not an end, 58
    multiple forms of, 19–20, 29
    ongoing, 28
    principles of, 65
    reform; *see* Reform
    review of, 60
    schedules, 59–64
    self-, 12, 20, 34–35, 42, 48, 59,
      60, 87, 104
    standardized, 20
    sustainability of, 186–187
    traditional, 183
    troubleshooting, 165–175

Benchmarking, 17–29, 44, 49
    age-related, 64

Checklists, 20, 42, 49
Children with disabilities, 55
Coalition of Essential Schools, 107
Community, 12, 13, 14, 31–37
Comparing, 17–29
Conferences, 13, 24, 41, 42, 58
    parent reactions to, 167–170
    parent-teacher, 49, 51, 59, 60,
      62, 63, 64, 89, 121–132, 133,
      157, 158
      during and after, 129–130
      formats for, 124–127

      preparing for, 127–129
      phases of, 122–123
      reactions to, 130–131
      reflections on, 131–132
    student-led, 15, 35, 49, 59, 60,
      61, 64, 131, 133–163
      after, 156–157
      components of, 136–146
      during, 156
      formats of, 147–154
      phases of, 134–136
      planning of, 155–156
      reactions to, 157–160
      troubleshooting at, 165–167
    student-teacher, 13, 51
    student-teacher-parent, 21
    teacher-led, 15, 35, 131
    videotaped portfolio, 35
Conversing, 17–29
Criticism, avoidance of, 42–43, 49,
    169
Curriculum, 62
    development, 65
    guides, 22, 24
    standards, 20, 33–34

Decision making, 43, 55
    guides in, 44
    quality, 55
    shared, 4–5, 11, 35, 39
    steps to, 40–56

Educational problem solving,
    174–175

Files,
    computer, 59
    teacher, 41

About the Authors

Rob Tierney turned his attention to "assessing assessment" and after several years of research and development efforts co-authored the first book on portfolio assessment for literacy educators. Since that time he has also written other significant articles on literacy assessment principles and practices which have been seminal. One of the most notable appeared in The Reading Teacher (Negotiating learner-based literacy assessments: Some guiding principles.) articles that have appeared in the Reading Research Quarterly " Negotiating issues of assessment, learning, and social justice as we approach the new millennium." & "Portfolios: assumptions, tensions, and possibilities" (with C. Clark). He is currently Dean of the faculty of Education at the University of British Columbia, but has held various faculty positions in the United States and retains strong ties with his homeland, Australia.

Thomas P. Crumpler is an assistant professor of reading and literacy at Illinois State University where he teaches courses in the assessment of reading, educational drama, and the assessment and education of teachers. His current research focuses on how portfolio-based assessment can help develop partnerships that inform literacy learning and the relationship between educational drama and the composing processes of young children.

His work has appeared in Research in Drama Education, Arts and Learning, The New Advocate, and other journals.

Cynthia D. Bertelsen received her M.A. and Ph.D. from The Ohio State University. Currently, she is an assistant professor in the Division of Teaching and Learning at Bowling Green State University (OH) where she teaches undergraduate and graduate literacy courses. Her research interests include literacy learning of young children, interdisciplinary literacy programs, inclusive education, learner-based assessments,and teacher preparation and professional development.

Ernest Bond is an Assistant Professor at Salisbury University in Salisbury, Maryland. Most of his research concerns interactive assessment, children's and young adult literature, and literacy and technology. Recent publications include "Rewriting Harry's World" in Harry Potter's World: Multidisciplinary Critical Perspectives (ed. Heilman Routledge, 2003), and an upcoming young adult literature textbook (Merrill/Prentice Hall). He has presented on various topics at AERA, IRA, NCTE, and NRC. He is also an active member of the ALA and YALSA.